The Living Dharma Series: Oral Teachings of
Chagdud Tulku

Gates to Buddhist Practice

Other books by Chagdud Tulku

Life in Relation to Death
Lord of the Dance

Gates to Buddhist Practice

Chagdud Tulku

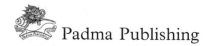 Padma Publishing

Published by Padma Publishing
P.O. Box 279
Junction City, CA 96048

© Padma Publishing 1993

Printed in the United States of America

Library of Congress Cataloging-in-Publication Data
Chagdud Tulku, 1930–
Gates to Buddhist practice / Chagdud Tulku.
p. cm. — (The living dharma series : Oral teachings of
Chagdud Tulku)
ISBN 1-881847-02-0
1. Religious life—Buddhism. 2. Buddhism. I. Title.
II. Series.
BQ5395.C43 1993
294.3'444—dc20   93-12969
                                                      CIP

ISBN 1-881847-02-0 Paperback

Contents

Series Preface

Gates to Buddhist Practice, the first volume of The Living Dharma Series: Oral Teachings of Chagdud Tulku, presents traditional Tibetan Buddhist wisdom to Western readers in Chagdud Tulku's uniquely accessible style, interweaving stories from his native Tibet with a step-by-step exploration of the foundation and essence of Vajrayana Buddhism.

Son of Dawa Drolma, one of Tibet's most renowned female lamas, Chagdud Tulku received extensive training from many great lamas and belongs to the last generation of teachers to have inherited the vast wealth of Tibetan Vajrayana teachings and methods before the Chinese Communist consolidation of power in Tibet. In 1959, he was forced into exile and, during the two decades that followed, served the Tibetan community in India and Nepal as lama and physician. He also aided in refugee resettlement, as well as the artistic development of new monasteries.

Abbott of Chagdud Gonpa in Tibet—a centuries-old monastery and one of the few to survive the Chinese Communist invasion—Chagdud Tulku came to the United States in 1979. In 1983 he established the Chagdud Gonpa Foundation, which currently has twelve centers in California, Oregon, Washington, Canada, and Brazil. Now a United States citizen, he lives at Chagdud Gonpa's main center in Trinity County, northern California, and continues to travel and teach extensively throughout the United

States, Asia, Europe, Australia, and South America. His wisdom and compassion, which derive from a treasury of human experience, scholarly training, and profound meditative insight, permeate his presentation of the Buddha-dharma—a presentation that, rich with metaphor, transcends cultural and religious barriers, and spirals through the extensive body of Buddhist teachings to their very heart.

Since Rinpoche came to the West, thousands of spiritual practitioners have gained insight into mind's nature through his instruction on the Vajrayana. A master of the most profound teachings of the Buddhist path, the Great Perfection (Dzogchen), he is committed to making the full range of Vajrayana methods available to students in the West. His teachings, imbued with the Great Perfection perspective and transmitted with warmth and humor, reveal to those who are receptive a glimpse of their intrinsic awareness.

Most of the public talks Rinpoche has given since his arrival in the West have been tape-recorded. The Living Dharma Series consists of edited transcripts of those teachings. In *Gates to Buddhist Practice,* Chagdud Tulku speaks of why we suffer and how we can eliminate the causes of suffering to create ultimate freedom for ourselves and others. He presents a multitude of methods for working with the mind in daily life; for reducing anger, attachment, ignorance, jealousy, and pride; for practicing effortful and effortless meditation; and for developing wisdom and compassion. *Gates to Buddhist Practice* illuminates and clarifies themes in Buddhist thought for both new and experienced readers, providing insight and instruction to people of all religious backgrounds and walks of life. Readers will find spiritual truths that are relevant to and of immediate benefit in their daily lives, truths that when applied with sincerity will produce unequivocal changes in their own minds and in their interactions with others. The book also contains an introduction to the Vajrayana, the "lightning path," which can be pursued with a qualified teacher.

The teachings presented here, edited to remove excessive repetition and approved by Rinpoche, serve as an introduction to his presentation of the Buddhadharma. Individual chapters are self-contained, yet the book proceeds through a progression of ideas, themes, and practices. Terms or ideas that may be new to readers are defined in context, and elaboration upon their meaning can be found with the help of the Index.

The depth of these teachings will become increasingly apparent upon repeated readings, but more so through the application of the principles taught. For *Gates to Buddhist Practice* is a book not only about the philosophy of the Buddhist religion, but also about Buddhist practice, the methods taught by the Buddha Shakyamuni 2,500 years ago that have produced profound transformation in the minds of those who have diligently applied them.

May this book be the cause of liberation for all who read it, and may all find freedom from the cycles of suffering and awaken to their mind's true nature.

Acknowledgments

It is because of Chagdud Tulku's tireless compassion, kindness, and commitment to the liberation of beings that these teachings have become available.

Great appreciation is due to the translators and interpreters of these teachings: Richard Barron, who translated from the Tibetan, and Tsering Everest, Lisa Leghorn, and Jane Tromge, who interpreted Rinpoche's new and unique English for Western audiences.

Extensive gratitude is extended to Mary Racine, Kimberly Snow, and Barry Spacks, who worked tirelessly as a team with Lisa Leghorn, series editor, to enable *Gates to Buddhist Practice* to emerge from the transcript pages, and again to Kimberly, who patiently, diligently, and meticulously inputted repeated manuscript drafts, as well as to Prema Swearingen, whose last-minute transcription and inputting were crucial to the book's publication. Many thanks also to Richard Baldwin, who edited portions of the material, and to Bob Tajima for the production of the book. Appreciation is due as well to the many transcriptionists, to those who read drafts and gave feedback, and to Jane Tromge, managing editor of Padma Publishing, for her support.

Part I

*Discovering the Path
to Freedom*

1 Turning the Wheel

Why do we need a spiritual path? We live in a busy age, our lives overflow with activities—some joyous, some painful, some satisfying, some not. Why take time to do spiritual practice?

A story is often told about a man from the northern region of Tibet who decided to go on a pilgrimage with his friends to the Potala Palace, the Dalai Lama's home in Lhasa, a very holy place. It was the trip of a lifetime.

In those days, there were no cars or vehicles of any kind in that region and people journeyed by foot or by horse. It took a long time to get anywhere, and it was dangerous to go very far, as many thieves and robbers preyed on unsuspecting travelers. For these reasons, most people never left their home area from birth to death. Most had never seen a house; they lived in black tents woven from yak hair fiber.

When this particular group of pilgrims finally arrived in Lhasa, the man from the north was awed by the multistoried Potala Palace with its many windows and the spectacular view of the town from within. He put his head through a narrow slit of a window to get a better look, twisting it left and right as he gazed at the sights below. When his friends called for him to leave, he jerked his head back, but couldn't get it out of the window. He became very nervous, pulling this way and that.

Finally he decided he was really stuck. So he said to his friends, "Go home without me. Tell my family the bad news is that I died, but the good news is that I died in the Potala Palace. What better place to die?"

His friends were also very simple-minded people, so without thinking much about it, they agreed and left. Some time later, the palace shrine keeper came along and asked, "Beggar, what are you doing here?"

"I'm dying," he answered.

"Why do you think you are dying?"

"Because my head is stuck."

"How did you get it in?"

"I just put it in like this."

The shrine keeper replied, "So pull it out the same way it went in!"

The man did as the shrine keeper suggested—and he was free.

Like this man, if we can see where we're caught, we can break free and help others to do the same. But first, we need to understand how we got where we are.

Throughout life, though each of us seeks, and sometimes finds, happiness, it is always temporary; we cannot make it last. It's as if we keep shooting arrows, but at the wrong target. To find long-lasting happiness, we need to change our target, to focus on eradicating the suffering of ourselves and others, not temporarily, but permanently.

The mind is the source of both our suffering and our happiness. It can be used positively to create benefit, or negatively to create harm. Although every being's fundamental nature is beginningless, deathless purity—what we call buddha nature—we don't recognize it. Instead, we are controlled by the whims of ordinary mind, which goes up and down, around and about, producing good and bad, pleasant and painful thoughts. Meanwhile, we plant a seed with every thought, word, and action. As surely as the seed of a poisonous plant produces poisonous fruit or a medicinal plant a cure, harmful actions produce suffering and beneficial actions, happiness.

Our actions become causes, and from causes naturally come results. Anything put into motion produces a corresponding motion. Throw a pebble into a pond and waves flow out in rings, strike the bank, and return. So it is when thoughts move: waves flow out, waves return. When the results of those thoughts come back, we feel like helpless victims: we're innocently leading our lives—why are all these things happening to us? What's happening is that the rings are coming back to the center. This is karma.

Ordinary mind is vacillating and full of turbulence. Without any power to control it and its effects on body and speech, we're up, then down, back and forth: it's like riding a roller coaster of reality. Actually it's closer to turning a wheel. We start a wheel turning, and every time we react, we give it another spin, and we're caught in its perpetual motion. In this way, our ever-cycling experience of reality, in all of its variations, continues lifetime after lifetime. This is the endlessness of samsara, of cyclic existence. We don't understand that we're experiencing results that we ourselves have brought into being and that our reactions produce more causes, more results—ceaselessly.

Because we ourselves created the predicament we're in, it's up to us to change it. Someone with matted, greasy hair looking in a mirror can't clean up his image by wiping the mirror. Someone with a bile disease will have a distorted sense of color, will see a white surface—whether a distant snow mountain or a piece of white cloth—as slightly yellow. The only way to correct that flawed vision is to cure the disease. Trying to change the external environment won't do any good.

Some people think the remedy for suffering lies with God or with Buddha, somewhere external to them. But that's not the case. The Buddha himself said to his disciples, "I have shown you the path to freedom. Following that path depends on you."

The mind, when used positively—to generate compassion, for example—can create great benefit. It may appear that this benefit comes from God or Buddha. But it is simply the result of the seeds we've planted. And although from the Buddha's teachings we receive the key of knowledge that allows us to change, tame, and train the mind, only we can unlock its deeper truth, exposing our buddha nature with its limitless capacities.

Our current experience is one of relative good fortune. There are many who suffer far worse than we do. Ravaged by the relentless pain of war, sickness, or famine, they have no way to change their situations; there seems to be no escape.

If we contemplate their predicament, compassion arises in our hearts. We become inspired not to waste our fortunate circumstances, but to use them to create benefit for ourselves and others, benefit beyond the temporary happiness that comes and goes in the endless cycles of samsaric suffering. Only by fully revealing mind's true nature—by attaining enlightenment—can we find an abiding happiness and help others to do the same. This is the goal of the spiritual path.

2 *Working with Attachment and Desire*

To understand how suffering arises, practice watching your mind. Begin by simply letting it relax. Without thinking of the past or the future, without feeling hope or fear about this thing or that, let it rest comfortably, open and natural. In this space of the mind, there is no problem, no suffering. Then something catches your attention—an image, a sound, a smell. Your mind splits into inner and outer, self and other, subject and object. In simply perceiving the object, there is still no problem. But when you zero in on it, you notice that it's big or small, white or black, square or circular; and then you make a judgment—for example, whether it's pretty or ugly. Having made that judgment, you react to it: you decide you like it or don't like it.

That's when the problem starts, because "I like it" leads to "I want it." Similarly, "I don't like it" leads to "I don't want it." If we like something, want it, and can't have it, we suffer. If we want it, get it, and lose it, we suffer. If we don't want it, but can't keep it away, again we suffer. Our suffering seems to occur because of the object of our desire or aversion, but that's not really so—it happens because the mind splits into object–subject duality and becomes involved in wanting or not wanting something.

We often think the only way to create happiness is to try to control the outer circumstances of our lives, to try to fix what seems wrong or to get rid of everything that bothers us. But the real problem lies in our reaction to those circumstances. What we have to change is the mind and the way it experiences reality.

Our emotions propel us through extremes, from elation to depression, from good experiences to bad, from happiness to sadness—a constant swinging back and forth. Emotionality is the by-product of hope and fear, attachment and aversion. We have hope because we are attached to something we want. We have fear because we are averse to something we don't want. As we follow our emotions, reacting to our experiences, we create karma—a perpetual motion that inevitably determines our future. We need to stop the extreme swings of the emotional pendulum so that we can find a place of centeredness.

When we first begin to work with the emotions, we apply the principle of iron cutting iron or diamond cutting diamond. We use thought to change thought. An angry thought can be antidoted by a compassionate one, while desire can be antidoted by the contemplation of impermanence.

In the case of attachment, begin by examining what it is you're attached to. For example, you might, after much effort, succeed in becoming famous, thinking this will make you happy. Then your fame triggers jealousy in someone, who tries to kill you. What you worked so hard to create is the cause of your own suffering. Or you might work very hard to become wealthy, thinking this will bring happiness, only to lose all your money. The loss of wealth in itself is not the source of suffering, only attachment to having it.

We can lessen attachment by contemplating impermanence. It is certain that whatever we're attached to will either change or be lost. A person may die or go away, a friend may become an enemy, a thief may steal our money. Even our body, to which we're most attached, will be gone one day. Knowing this not only helps to reduce our attachment, but gives us a greater appreciation of what we have while we have it. For example, there is nothing wrong with money in itself, but if we're attached to it, we'll suffer when we lose it. Instead, we can appreciate it while it lasts, enjoy it and enjoy sharing it with others, and at the same time know it's impermanent. Then when we lose it, the emotional pendulum won't make as wide a swing toward sadness.

Imagine two people who buy the same kind of watch on the same day at the same shop. The first person thinks, "This is a very nice watch. It will be helpful to me, but it may not last long." The second person thinks, "This is the best watch I've ever had. No matter what happens, I can't lose it or let it break." If both people lose their watch, the one who is attached will be much more upset than the other.

If we are fooled by life and invest great value in one thing or another, we may find ourselves fighting for what we want and against any opposition. We may think that what we're fighting for is lasting, true, and real, but it's not. It's impermanent, it's not true, it's not lasting, and ultimately, it's not even real.

Our life can be compared to an afternoon at a shopping center. We walk through the shops, led by our desires, taking things off the shelves and tossing them in our baskets. We wander around, looking at everything, wanting and longing. We see a person or two, maybe smile and continue on, never to see them again.

Driven by desire, we don't appreciate the preciousness of what we already have. We need to realize that this time with our loved ones, our friends, our family, our co-workers is very brief. Even if we lived to a hundred and fifty, that would be very little time to enjoy and utilize our human opportunity.

Young people think their lives will be long; old people think life will end soon. But we can't assume these things. Our life comes with a built-in expiration date. There are many strong and healthy people who die young, while many of the old and sick and feeble live on and on. Not knowing when we'll die, we need to develop an appreciation for and acceptance of what we have, while we have it, rather than continuing to find fault with our experience and seeking, incessantly, to fulfill our desires.

If we start worrying whether our nose is too big or too small, we should think, "What if I had no head—now that would be a problem!" As long as we have life, we should rejoice. If everything doesn't go exactly as we'd like, we can accept it. If we contemplate impermanence deeply, patience and compassion will arise. We will hold less to the apparent truth of our experience, and the mind will become more flexible. Realizing that one day this body will be buried or burned, we will rejoice in every moment we have rather than make ourselves or others unhappy.

Now we are afflicted by "me-my-mine-itis," a condition caused by ignorance. Our self-centeredness and self-important thinking have become very strong habits. In order to change them, we need to refocus. Instead of concerning ourselves with "I" all the time, we must redirect our attention to "you" or "them" or "others." Reducing self-importance lessens the attachment that stems from it. When we focus outside ourselves, ultimately we realize the equality of ourselves and all other beings. Everybody wants happiness; nobody wants to suffer. Our attachment to our own happiness expands to an attachment to the happiness of all.

Until now, our desires have tended to be very short term, superficial, and selfish. If we are going to wish for something, let it be nothing less than complete enlightenment for all beings. That's something worthy of desire. Continually reminding ourselves of what is truly worth wanting is an important element of spiritual practice.

Desire and attachment won't change overnight. But desire becomes less ordinary as we redirect our worldly yearning toward the aspiration to do everything we can to help all beings find unchanging happiness. We don't have to abandon the ordinary objects of our desires—relationships, wealth, fame—but as we contemplate their impermanence, we become less attached to them. Rejoicing in our good fortune when they arise, yet recognizing that they won't last, we begin to develop spiritual qualities. We commit fewer of the harmful actions that result from attachment, and hence create less negative karma; we generate more fortunate karma, and mind's positive qualities gradually increase.

Eventually, as our meditation practice matures, we can try an approach that's different from contemplation, different from using thought to change thought: revealing the deeper nature, or wisdom principle, of the emotions as they arise.

If you are in the midst of a desire attack—something has captured your mind and you must have it—you won't get rid of the desire by trying to suppress it. Instead, you can begin to see through desire by examining what it is. When it arises in the mind, ask yourself, "Where does it come from? Where does it dwell? Can it be described? Does it have any color, shape, or form? When it disappears, where does it go?"

This is an interesting situation. You can say that desire exists, but if you search for the experience, you can't quite grasp it. On the other hand, if you say it doesn't exist, you're denying the obvious fact that you are feeling desire. You can't say that it exists, nor can you say that it does not exist. You can't say that it's "both" or "neither," that it both does exist and does not exist, or that it neither exists nor does not *not* exist. This is the meaning of the true nature of desire beyond the extremes of conceptual mind.

It's our failure to understand the essential nature of an emotion as it arises that gets us into trouble. Once we do, the emotion tends to dissolve. Then we're neither repressing nor encouraging it. We are simply looking clearly at what is taking place. If we set a cloudy glass of water aside for a while, it will settle by itself and become clear. Instead of judging the experience of desire, we look directly at its nature, what is known as "liberating it in its own ground."

Each negative emotion, or mental poison, has an inherent purity that we don't recognize because we are so accustomed to its appearance as emotion. The true nature of the five poisons—ignorance, attachment, aversion, jealousy, and pride—is the five wisdoms. Just as poison can be taken medicinally to effect a cure, each poison of the mind, worked with properly, can be resolved into its wisdom nature and thus enhance our spiritual practice.

If while in the throes of desire, you simply relax, without moving your attention, that space of the mind is called discriminating wisdom. You don't abandon desire—instead you reveal its wisdom nature.

Question: I'm not sure I understand what you mean by "liberating an emotion in its own ground."
Response: Our habit, when an emotion arises, is to become involved in analyzing and reacting to the apparent cause: the outer object. If, instead, we simply—without attachment or aversion, hatred or involvement—peel open the emotion, we will reveal and experience its wisdom nature. When we are feeling puffed up and on top of the world, instead of

either indulging in our pride or pushing it away, we relax the mind and reveal the intrinsic nature of pride as the wisdom of equanimity.

In working with the emotions we can apply different methods. When our mind is steeped in duality, in object–subject perception, we can cut iron with iron: we antidote a negative thought with a positive one, attachment to our own happiness with attachment to the happiness of others. If we are able to relax the dualistic habit of the mind, we can experience the true essence, or "ground," of an emotion and thus "liberate it in its own ground." In this way, its wisdom principle is revealed: pride as the wisdom of equanimity; jealousy as all-accomplishing wisdom; attachment and desire as discriminating wisdom; anger and aversion as mirror-like wisdom; and ignorance as dharmadhatu wisdom, the wisdom of the true nature of reality.

Question: Can you say more about how contemplating impermanence reduces attachment?

Response: Imagine a child and an adult on the beach building a sand castle. The adult has never taken the sand castle to be permanent or real, and isn't attached to it. When a wave comes in and washes it away or some other children come along and kick it down, the adult doesn't suffer. But the child has begun to think of it as a real house that will last forever, and so suffers when it's lost.

Like the child, we have pretended for so long that our experience is stable and reliable that we have great attachment to it and suffer when it changes. If we maintain an awareness of impermanence, then we are never completely fooled by the phenomena of samsara.

If you contemplate the fact that you don't have long to live, it will help you. You'll think, "In the time that I have left, why follow this anger or attachment, which will only produce more confusion and delusion? If I take what's impermanent so seriously and try to grasp it or push it away, then I'm only imagining as solid what isn't solid. I'm only further complicating, and perpetuating, the delusions of samsara. I won't do that! I'll use this attachment or this aversion, this pride or this jealousy, as practice." Spiritual practice doesn't only mean sitting on a meditation cushion. When you're there with the experience of desire or anger, right there where the mind is active, that is where you practice, at each moment, each step of your life.

Question: In contemplating impermanence I find my attachment lessening to a certain extent, but I wonder how far I should go in dropping things.

Response: You need to be discriminating in what you address first. Eventually you may drop everything, but begin by abandoning the mind's poisons—for example, anger. Instead of thinking, "Why wash these dishes, they're impermanent?" let go of your anger at having to do them. Also understand that whatever arises in the mind that sparks your anger is impermanent. The anger itself is impermanent. Whatever someone says to you that affects you in a negative way, that too is impermanent. Realize that these are only words, sounds, not something lasting.

The next thing to drop is attachment to having your own way. When you understand impermanence, it doesn't matter so much if things are going as you think they should. If they are, it's all right. If not, that's all right, too.

When you practice like this, the mind will slowly develop more balance. It won't flip one way or the other according to whether or not you get what you want.

Question: Is there anything wrong with being happy or sad, with feeling our emotions?

Response: Reminding ourselves when we experience happiness that it's impermanent, that it will eventually disappear, will help us to cherish and enjoy it while it lasts.

At the same time, we won't become so attached to it or fixated on it, and we won't experience as much pain when it's gone.

In the same way, when we experience pain, sorrow, or loss, we should remind ourselves that these things, too, are impermanent, which will alleviate our suffering. So what keeps us balanced is our ongoing awareness of impermanence.

Question: Is the self still involved as we expand the focus of our attachment to the needs of others?

Response: If you were bound with ropes tied in many knots, in order to become free you would have to release the knots, one by one, in the opposite order in which they were originally tied. First you'd release the last knot, then the second to the last, and so forth, until you undid the first, the one closest to you.

We're bound by many knots, including many kinds of attachment. Ideally we would have no clinging at all, but since that's not the case, we use attachment to cut attachment. We begin by untying the last knot: by replacing attachment to our own needs and desires with attachment to the happiness of others.

We need to understand that selfish attachment will sooner or later create problems. If you are attached to your own needs and desires, if you like to be happy and don't like to suffer, when something minor goes wrong it will seem gigantic. You will focus on it morning to night, exacerbating the problem. A crack in a teacup will begin to seem like the Grand Canyon after examination under the microscope of your constant attention.

This self-focusing is itself a kind of meditation. Meditation means bringing something back to the mind again and again. If we repeat virtuous thoughts and rest in mind's nature, this can lead to enlightenment. But self-important meditation will only produce endless suffering. Focusing on our problems may even result in suicide, because we can become so preoccupied with our suffering that life seems unbearable and without purpose. Suicide is the worst of solutions because such extreme attachment to death and aversion to human life can close the door to future human rebirth.

So we need to begin by reducing our self-focus and self-important thoughts. To do so, we remind ourselves that we aren't the only ones who want to be happy—everyone does. Though others seek happiness, they may not understand how to go about accomplishing it, whereas if we have some understanding of the spiritual path, we can perhaps help and support them in their efforts.

We remind ourselves that of course we'll encounter problems. We're humans. But though difficulties arise, we mustn't give them any power. Everyone has problems, many far worse than our own. As we contemplate this, our view expands to encompass the suffering of others. As our compassion deepens, our relentless self-focusing is reduced; we become more intent on helping others and better able to do so.

If we are physically sick, it's useful to be attached to the medicine that will make us well. However, once we're cured, that attachment needs to be cut. Otherwise the very medicine that cured us could make us sick again. Now we use the medicine of attachment to benefiting others in order to cut our self-attachment. We employ attachment to change attachment. Eventually, if we are to attain enlightenment, attachment itself must be cut.

3 Working with Anger and Aversion

Attachment and anger are two sides of the same coin. Because of ignorance and the mind's split into object–subject duality, we grasp at or push away what we perceive as external to us. When we encounter something we want and can't get, or someone prevents us from achieving what we've told ourselves we must achieve, or something happens that doesn't accord with the way we want things to be, we experience anger, aversion, or hatred. But these responses serve no benefit. They only cause harm. From anger, along with attachment and ignorance, the three poisons of the mind, we generate endless karma, endless suffering.

It is said that there is no evil like anger: by its very nature, anger is destructive, an enemy. Since not a shred of happiness ever comes from it, anger is one of the most potent negative forces.

Anger and aversion can lead to aggression. When harmed, many people feel they should retaliate by taking an eye for an eye. It's a natural response. "If someone speaks harshly to me, then I'll speak harshly in return. If someone hits me, I'll hit him back. That's what he deserves." Or, more extreme: "This person is my enemy. If I kill him, I'll be happy!"

We don't realize that if we have a tendency toward aversion and aggression, enemies start appearing everywhere. We find less and less to like about others, and more and more to hate. People begin to avoid us, and we become

17

more isolated and lonely. Sometimes, enraged, we spit out rough, abusive language. The Tibetans have a saying: "Words may not carry weapons, but they wound the heart." Our words can be extremely harmful both through the damage they do to others and the anger they evoke. Very often a cycle develops: one person feels aversion toward another and says something hurtful; the other person reacts by saying something out of line. The two start fueling each other until they're waging a battle of angry words. This can be extended, of course, to the national and international levels, where groups of people get caught up in aggression toward other groups, and nations are pitted against nations.

When you give in to aversion and anger, it's as though, having decided to kill someone by throwing him into a river, you wrap your arms around his neck, jump into the water with him, and you both drown. In destroying your enemy, you destroy yourself as well.

It is far better to defuse anger before it can lead to further conflict, by responding to it with patience. Understanding our own responsibility for what happens to us helps us to do so. Now we treat our connection with a perceived enemy as if it came out of nowhere. But in some previous existence, perhaps we spoke harshly to that person, physically abused or harbored angry thoughts about him. Instead of finding fault with others, directing anger and aversion at situations and people we think are threatening us, we should address the true enemy. That enemy, which destroys our short-term happiness and prevents us, in the long term, from attaining enlightenment, is our own anger and aversion.

Then the confrontation comes to nothing. There is no fight, you no longer perceive the person you've been confronting as an enemy, and the true enemy has been vanquished—a great return for a little bit of effort. In the long run, both you and the other person are less likely to get repeatedly into situations where conflict could develop. You both benefit.

Our habitual tendency is to contemplate in counterproductive ways. If someone insults us, we usually dwell on it, asking ourselves, "Why did he say that to me?" and on and on. It's as if someone shoots an arrow at us, but it falls short. Focusing on the problem is like picking the arrow up and repeatedly stabbing ourselves with it, saying, "He hurt me so much. I can't believe he did that."

Instead, we can use the method of contemplation to think things through differently, to change our habit of reacting with anger. Since it is difficult at first to think clearly in the midst of an altercation, we begin by practicing at home, alone, imagining confrontations and new ways of responding. Imagine, for example, that someone insults you. He's disgusted with you, slaps you, or offends you in some way. You think, "What should I do? I'll defend myself—I'll retaliate. I'll throw him out of my house." Now try another approach. Say to yourself, "This person makes me angry. But what is anger? It is one of the poisons of the mind that generates negative karma, leading to intense suffering. Meeting anger with anger is like following a lunatic who jumps off a cliff. Do I have to do likewise? If it's crazy for him to act the way he does, it's even crazier for me to act the same way."

Remember that those who are acting aggressively toward you are only buying their own suffering, creating their own worse predicament, through ignorance. They think that they're doing what's best for themselves, that they're correcting something that's wrong, or preventing something worse from happening. But the truth is that their behavior will be of no benefit. They are in many ways like a person with a headache beating his head with a hammer to try to stop the pain. In their unhappiness, they blame others, who in turn become angry and fight, only making matters worse. When we consider their predicament, we realize they should be the object of our compassion rather than our blame and anger. Then we aspire to do what we can to protect them from further suffering, as we would a child who keeps misbehaving, running again and again into the road, hitting and scratching us as we attempt to bring her back. Instead of giving up on those who cause harm, we need to realize that they are seeking happiness but don't know how to find it.

The role of enemy isn't a permanent one. The person hurting you now might be a best friend later. Your enemy now could even, in a former lifetime, have been the one who gave birth to you, the mother who fed and took care of you.

By contemplating again and again in this way, we learn to respond to aggression with compassion and answer anger with kindness.

Another approach we can use is to develop awareness of the illusory quality of our anger and the object of our anger. If, for example, someone says to you, "You're a bad person," ask yourself, "Does that make me bad? If I were a bad person and someone said I was good, would that make me good?" If someone says coal is gold, does it become gold? If someone says gold is coal, does it become coal? Things don't change just because someone says this or that. Why take such talk so seriously?

Sit in front of a mirror, look at your refection, and insult it: "You're ugly. You're bad." Then praise it: "You're beautiful. You're good." Regardless of what you say, the image remains simply what it is. Praise and blame are not real in and of themselves. Like an echo, a shadow, a mere reflection, they hold no power to help or harm us.

As we practice in this way, we begin to realize that things lack solidity, like a dream or illusion. We develop a more spacious state of mind—one that isn't so reactive. Then when anger arises, instead of responding immediately, we can look back on it and ask: "What is this? What is making me turn red and shake? Where is it?" What we discover is that there is no substance to anger, no *thing* to find.

Once we realize we can't find anger, we can let the mind be. We don't suppress the anger, push it away, or engage it. We simply let the mind rest in the midst of it. We can stay with the energy itself—simply, naturally, remaining aware of it, without attachment, without aversion. Then we find that anger, like desire, isn't really what we thought it was. We begin to see its nature, to realize its essence, which is mirror-like wisdom.

It may sound easy to do this, but it's not. Anger stimulates us and we fly—one way or the other. We fly in our mind, we fly off to a judgment, we fly to a reaction, we fly to this or that, becoming involved with whatever has upset us. Our habit of lashing back in this way has been reinforced again and again, lifetime after lifetime. If our understanding of the essence of anger is only superficial, we'll find out that we aren't capable of applying it to real-life situations.

There is a famous Tibetan folk tale of a man meditating in retreat. Somebody came to see him and asked, "What are you meditating on?"

"Patience," he said.

"You're a fool!"

This made the meditator furious and he immediately started an argument—which proved exactly how much patience he had.

Only through continual, methodical application of these methods, day by day, month by month, year by year, will we dissolve our deeply ingrained habits. The process may take some time, but we *will* change. Look how quickly we change in negative ways. We're quite happy, and then somebody says or does something and we get irritated. Changing in a positive way requires discipline, exertion, and patience. The word for "meditation" in Tibetan is a cognate of the verb "to become familiar with" or "to acclimatize." Using a variety of methods, we become familiar with other ways of being.

There's an expression: "Even an elephant can be tamed in various ways." When goads or hooks are used skillfully, this enormous, powerful beast can be led along very gently. It is said that when elephants are decorated for festive occasions, they become docile, moving as though they were walking on eggshells. Or if they're in a large crowd of people, elephants are very easily controlled. So something that is big and unwieldy can actually be managed well with the proper means. In the same way, the mind, often unwieldy and wild, can be tamed with skillful methods.

The difference between a worldly person's approach to life and that of a spiritual practitioner is that the worldly person always looks at phenomena as if through a window, judging the outer experience, while the practitioner uses experience as a mirror to repeatedly examine his or her own mind in minute detail, to determine where the strengths and weaknesses lie, how to develop the one and eliminate the other.

We don't need a psychic to tell us what our future experience will be—we need only look at our own minds. If we have a good heart and helpful intentions toward others, we will continually find happiness. If, instead, the mind is filled with ordinary self-centered thoughts, with anger and harmful intentions toward others, we will find only difficult experiences.

If we check the mind again and again, continuously applying antidotes to the poisons that arise, we will slowly see change. Only we ourselves can really know what is taking place in the mind. It's easy to lie to others. We can pretend that a thick leather bag is full, but as soon as someone sits on it, he'll know whether it's truly full. Similarly, we can sit for hours in meditation posture, but if poisonous thoughts circulate in the mind all the while, we're only pretending to do spiritual practice. Instead, we can be honest with ourselves, taking responsibility for what we see in our own minds instead of judging others, and apply the appropriate remedy for change.

Question: Is it wrong for me to feel anger toward those responsible for war, for hurting so many?

Response: In the act of killing, the person who kills is as worthy of our compassion as the person who is killed. The person killed is fulfilling a karmic debt which has led to the cutting off of his life, and in that act, that karma is purified. The person inflicting the death is sowing seeds for future suffering on an enormous scale, far greater than that of his victim, and he doesn't even realize it. Surely both the victim and aggressor deserve our compassion.

One of our strongest concerns today is the attainment of world peace, an end toward which many groups and individuals struggle, an activity entirely noble in intention. However, if aggression is involved, if we are *fighting* for peace, if one group says to another, "You're not making peace in the world so we're going to get rid of you," we are only fueling the anger that gave rise to the lack of peace in the first place. Instead, we need to develop compassion and helpfulness in all directions.

Our efforts to create world peace will depend on how we as individuals react to situations. If we express anger, hatred, aversion, aggression, we will only exacerbate the problem. So it's important not only to cultivate noble ideals, but to uphold and embody them throughout our lives.

4 Working with Ignorance

In tracing back the causes of our confusion and suffering, we come to the fundamental problem of basic ignorance. The reason we suffer as we do, the reason we encounter the problems we do, the reason we continue to wander in samsara, cyclic existence, is that we are unaware of our true nature. This lack of recognition has a dynamic quality that expresses itself in our projection and experience of the phenomenal world, which appears to us as solid, composed of the various elements. We are continually under the impression that there is an "I" poised against everything else that isn't "I." Because of this dualistic tendency of the mind, we objectify our experience and make judgments about the objects we perceive; this leads to attachment and aversion, which generate karma and endless suffering. Dualistic clinging, emotional confusion, habit, karma, and the fruits of karma are all natural consequences of this lack of awareness.

Because we don't know the true nature of our body, speech, or mind, our environment, the past or the future, we take daily events to be true, just as when we are dreaming we take our dreams to be true. When we dream at night, in a sense we're confused because we believe that we're actually in a particular place, doing certain things: maybe driving a car, building something, even running from a tiger.

In the dream we remember the past and can project a

future. Sky, ground, breathing, swallowing—everything seems real. Actually, we're asleep in bed and nothing is really happening. Yet while we dream, our reality is dream reality. If a dream-tiger chases us, we run as fast as we can to save our life.

Once we wake up, or become aware in the dream that we're dreaming, our confusion disappears. The tiger has no more power, we're no longer afraid of it, because we realize that the whole experience was created by our own mind. As long as we're dreaming and remain in the grip of confusion, hope and fear persist; the consequences seem crucial. But when the knowledge that we're dreaming dispels our confusion, there's no more hope or fear.

In actuality, all existence, whether the suffering of samsara or the blissful experience of nirvana, is as insubstantial as our dreams. All of it is unreal, untrue. It's an unceasing, luminous, magnificent, illusory display.

Our life from birth to death resembles one long dream. And each dream we have at night is a dream within a dream. Perhaps you've experienced dreaming at night and then waking up and telling somebody, "I had an amazing dream." You make coffee, you're ready to go to work, and suddenly the alarm goes off and you really wake up. You hadn't been awake before at all. You'd only dreamed you were awake. This is called a false awakening, a dream of waking, and it's what we do every morning of our lives. In the dream of life we think we're awake, but in fact we're still dreaming. It's just that the alarm clock hasn't sounded yet.

We're dreamers and we experience short dreams of the night within this long dream of life, within the even longer dream of samsaric becoming. We've been taught and assume our daily experience is real and true, so when something difficult happens, we suffer. We've also been taught that our dreams are an illusion, so we tend to suffer less from our nightmares than from the events in our daily lives. The dream world comes and goes, it's clearly impermanent, so we think it's not real. Yet the same is true of our daily reality. It, too, is impermanent. The only difference between them is how long they last.

To know that our reality is not the whole truth of existence frees us from suffering. We're no longer controlled by our fears or our attachments. Yet the mind easily falls back into its old assumptions with the next movement of this daytime dream. Suddenly a lovely woman or a wonderful man appears, and there we are, believing in the dream we call reality once more. We've been fooled again; the illusion hasn't been completely dispelled—it only trembled for a second. We briefly realized the deeper nature of our experience, but the realization didn't hold.

We need a method for remembering that we're only dreaming, for truly breaking through our confusion, not just glimpsing the truth in one moment and forgetting it the next. We need, clearly and decisively, to bring our deluded experience of reality to an end. This requires an authentic recognition of the truth of our experience. Like the true nature of the night dream, it is beyond the extremes of conceptual thought, of "is" and "is not," and cannot be grasped by the rational mind.

Suppose we discover a big piece of gold and fail to recognize its value. Our lack of recognition doesn't make it of less worth in the slightest way. Nor does thinking that it has value increase its worth. It simply is what it is. If we know its value, we will use it appropriately. If we don't, we might use it to hold open a screen door or to prop up a big book. The gold wouldn't be functioning to its greatest potential.

The foundational nature of the mind is already gold; we simply don't recognize it as such. The fruit of the spiritual path is the complete realization of the gold; the path is how we accomplish that goal, making obvious what already exists.

In the method of meditation called dream yoga, the first task is to realize, during the dream, that we are dreaming. The next task is to maintain this realization, at which point we acquire a creative capacity in the dream. Say you were dreaming of a single balloon. If you could fully maintain your understanding of the nature of the dream, you could make many more balloons appear. Or a single person could become many; this world could become a different one. In short, we gain the capacity to increase, multiply, travel in dreams because the falsity of the dream no longer commands us. With recognition of its nature, we command the dream.

It is exactly the same in our daytime reality, from the moment we're born until we die. Many people have come to a realization of the true nature of this life's experience. In the Buddhist tradition, they're called *mahasiddhas*. In other traditions as well, people have attained such great realization that ordinary rules of reality failed to bind them. For example, Jesus walked on water. Great realized ones can leave footprints in solid stone or fly through the sky. What is hot to us is not hot to them, what's cold, not cold, nor solid, solid. They command reality; it does not command them.

To know the true nature of our experience, and to maintain that knowing, is the means of attaining enlightenment. Enlightenment is not anything new. It's not something we create or bring into existence. Enlightenment means simply discovering within us what is already there. It is the full realization of our own intrinsic nature, called buddha or, in Tibetan, *sang gyay*. *Sang* means "faultless," while *gyay* means "full realization"; just as from darkness, the moon waxes, likewise from ignorance, the qualities of the mind's intrinsic nature emerge.

Like water, which is fluid in its natural state but turns to ice when frozen, the true nature of mind—which can be called God, Buddha, perfection—appears differently when obscured by confusion and delusion. Buddha hasn't gone anywhere, just as the water hasn't gone anywhere. When the ice melts, the water regains its natural qualities. When mind's obscurations are removed, the truth of our nature becomes apparent.

But now, bound by our belief in the dream we call life, we can't see our true nature. As dreamers, however, we have choices; we can create good life dreams or bad ones. If we wish to make them good, we must change. Otherwise, the mind, left to its old habits, will not necessarily create better dreams.

We can also choose not to dream but instead to wake up. To awaken fully means to recognize the greater truth, the intrinsic, pure nature of body, speech, and mind. If we want to wake up, however, we won't automatically emerge from our deep sleep. We need methods, and we need to apply them.

Wisdom—knowing our true nature—is a direct antidote to ignorance, not knowing. It is the lamp that dispels the darkness of our minds. The Buddhist path brings us to a place of wisdom knowing instead of the ordinary knowing that informs our everyday activities.

We gain wisdom in three ways. First, someone who understands more than we do introduces us to something greater than anything we've known. But hearing this teaching, even in detail, isn't enough to engender belief in what we've learned. Blind faith in itself isn't very valuable, because first we have to understand what we're being taught. Then we can harness all our abilities to our practice.

Second, after having heard the teachings in great detail, we think about them, bringing our intellect and intelligence to bear, reflecting, questioning, examining to see if what we have been taught is true, to see if it works. In this process of contemplation, questions arise. We ask them, get answers, and then contemplate again. If we don't research and probe, if we don't remove doubt, then doing spiritual practice will be like trying to sew with a two-pointed needle. We won't get very far. Through contemplation, we come to a place of deep comprehension, a certainty that is the result of contemplative wisdom, as opposed to intellectual wisdom, the mere amassing of facts.

Finally, when we apply that contemplative wisdom to our experience again and again, it becomes more intuitive and we begin to develop meditative wisdom. Meditation is crucial to removing ignorance, because even deep understanding can be forgotten. Through meditation our inherent wisdom becomes completely obvious.

5 *Daily Life as Spiritual Practice*

As a way of introducing the topic of meditation in daily life, I'd like to draw on some of my own experiences and training in Tibet. There, at the age of two, I was recognized as a *tulku,* one who has directed successive rebirths for the benefit of others. This means that I was expected to turn out rather special. By the age of five I'd been taught to read and write. I had my own tutor, which in one way was very fortunate, because every day, all day, someone sat in attendance teaching me. On the other hand, whenever I made a mistake or forgot a lesson, I encountered the swing of the stick.

Even as a very young child I found myself exposed to profound spiritual teachings, either in a group or just one on one with my tutor. I studied the nature of absolute and relative truth. And it was then that I first encountered the truth of impermanence. Once our universe wasn't here. Slowly it came into being, and over time it will age and at some point dissipate. Even our own body wasn't here at one time. Each day it ages and some day it will cease to be. Everything in our experience is subject to impermanence. Recognizing this truth is foundational to developing a spiritual perspective.

When I first encountered this teaching, I resisted it strongly; I simply didn't want to hear it. I thought, yes, of course, seasons change, people change, lives change—who cares? I didn't pay a lot of attention to it. But by the age of nine, after I'd heard this teaching again and again, I'd begun to contemplate impermanence, having by then gained a little realization of its nature.

Understanding impermanence didn't change things for me drastically at first. I experienced just a little less grasping, a little less desire and attachment to the things in life we normally become attached to. The change was a very subtle one, based on the realization that things weren't quite as real as they had previously seemed to be.

That shift in perspective was tremendously helpful at the time my mother died, when I was only eleven years old. It also helped when I was twelve and my brother died, and at thirteen when my very dear guardian and teacher had to leave. Those experiences of death and separation were not easy, but the shift in perception that came from contemplating impermanence made them less unbearable. And later this perspective helped when I had to face the loss of my monastery and my country.

I learned that the more attached we are to our possessions and relationships in the world, the more important and necessary we think they are, the more pain we experience when they cease to be. For this reason alone, it's crucial to contemplate impermanence.

It's also very important to understand the good fortune of having a human body. Most of us take human existence lightly, too much for granted; we become callous to the natural joy of having a human form. We may not all have the eye of wisdom, but those who do tell us about realms of experience other than our own. Yet the greatest opportunity of all is that of a human birth. In another realm we may get a body that's seemingly more pleasant, but we will never be able to accomplish what we can as a human. We simply won't have the capability.

Sometimes people fail to realize what an incomparable opportunity we have because their lives are disappointing or very trying, and they lose interest in taking advantage of their human capacities. That is a grave mistake. The chances this body provides, right now, are far too great to be overlooked because of disappointment or difficulty.

It's as if you borrowed a boat to cross a river, and instead of using it right away, you took your time, forgetting that it wasn't yours but was only loaned to you. If you didn't take advantage of it while you had it, you'd never get across the river, for sooner or later the borrowed boat would be reclaimed, the opportunity lost.

This human body is a rare vehicle, and we need to use it well, without delay. The most exalted purpose of a precious human birth is to advance spiritually. If we are not able to travel far, at least we can make some progress; even better, we can help others to progress. As a very minimum, we mustn't make other people miserable.

We don't have much time in life. It's like a picnic on a Sunday afternoon. Just to look at the sun, to see things growing, to breathe the fresh air is a joy. But if all we do is fight about where to put the blanket, who's going to sit on which corner, who gets the wing or the drumstick, what a waste! Sooner or later, rain clouds come, dark approaches, and the picnic's finished. And all we've done is fight and bicker. Think of what we've lost.

You might wonder: if everything is impermanent, nothing is lasting, how can anyone live happily? It's true that we can't really grasp and hold onto things, but we can use that knowledge to look at life differently, as a very brief and precious opportunity. If we bring to our lives the maturity of knowing that everything is impermanent, we will find that our experiences are richer, our relationships more sincere, that we have greater appreciation for what we already enjoy.

We'll also be more patient. We'll realize that no matter how bad things might seem now, such unfortunate circumstances cannot last. We'll feel we can endure them until they pass. And with greater patience, we'll be more gentle with those around us. It's not so hard to extend a loving gesture once we realize that we may never see a great aunt again. Why not make her happy? Why not take the time to listen to all those old stories?

Coming to an understanding of impermanence and a genuine desire to make others happy in this brief opportunity we have together represents the beginning of true spiritual practice. It is this kind of sincerity that truly catalyzes transformation of mind and being. We don't have to shave our heads or wear special robes. We don't have to leave home or sleep on a bed of stone. Spiritual practice doesn't require austere conditions, only a good heart and the maturity to comprehend impermanence. This will lead to progress.

If we only make a show of spirituality, burning the right incense, sitting the right way, speaking the right words, we're liable to become more proud, more self-righteous, condescending, and faultfinding. Such false practice won't help us or others at all. The purpose of spiritual practice is not to increase our faults.

Having heard this once, we may become inspired. It makes us warm inside, makes us happy, to hear such truths. But it's a bit like patching a hole in our clothes: if we don't sew the patch on well, pretty soon it's going to start slipping and the hole's going to show again.

This is where we come to contemplation and meditation. Even though we can be inspired and touched by the simplicity and profundity of a spiritual approach to life, still our habits are very strong and the world remains difficult for us to contend with. Effective practice requires a constant reiteration of what we know to be true.

Meditation is a process of stitching, of reminding ourselves again and again of the deeper truths—impermanence, loving kindness—until the patch is sewn on so strongly that it becomes a part of the cloth and strengthens the whole garment.

Then we're not shaken by outer circumstances. There is a kind of ease that comes when we understand the illusory nature of reality, when we comprehend the dreamlike quality of life, this impermanence that pervades everything. Even as it is it isn't, and someday it won't be at all. This doesn't mean that we deny our involvement with life, but that we don't take it quite so seriously; we approach it with less hope and fear. Then we're like the adult playing with the child on the beach: the adult doesn't suffer as the child does if the sand castle is washed out to sea. Yet compassion arises for the child's suffering.

Compassion is natural to every one of us, but because we have deep, very self-centered habits, we need to cultivate it by contemplating the suffering of those who invest their dream with solidity. We need to develop a sincere, compassionate desire that their suffering will cease, that they will come to understand the dreamlike quality of life and thus avoid agony over the inevitable loss of things they value.

For twelve years, a very great Indian scholar and practitioner, Atisha, studied many texts, huge bodies of teachings and commentaries on the doctrine of the Buddha and the realizations of great lamas. After his years of study, he came to the conclusion that every single method—and the

Buddha taught 84,000 methods for achieving the transition from ordinary to extraordinary mind—came down to the essential point of good-heartedness.

When we merely talk about purity of heart it seems simple, but in difficult times it's not so easy to maintain. If you are face to face with someone who hates you, someone who would hurt you, it's very hard not to become angry and lose your loving kindness.

It is taught by the Buddha and by beings of infallible wisdom who know all causes and conditions of the past, present, and future that we have all had countless lifetimes. This may prove difficult for some of us to accept, because of course we haven't achieved so high a degree of wisdom: we don't know where we came from before we were born or where we will go after we die. But if we think about it, we live in the midst of today as a consequence of having had a yesterday, and similarly today supplies the basis for our having a tomorrow. It's the same with the sequence of existence. We have this life, which means there was some previous basis for it, while the present itself forms the ground for what will occur next.

If our inherent wisdom were more fully revealed, we'd see that all beings—whether human, animal, or otherwise—at some time throughout countless lifetimes have shown us the kindness of parents, given us a body, protected us, enabled us to survive, provided education, understanding, and some sort of worldly training. It doesn't matter what their roles are now or how difficult our relationships with them may be. It's as if we are playing at make-believe. We're like actors who come to believe we're actually the characters we're enacting.

When we understand this connection between ourselves and every other being, equanimity arises. We regard everyone, whether friend or foe, with consideration. Even though someone may prove difficult, it doesn't mean that person hasn't been important to us before.

When we see one who has once been our parent suffering terribly, our compassion deepens. We contemplate, "How sad—she doesn't understand. If I understand a little bit more, it's my responsibility to help her as much as I can."

A perception like that softens us. Then, when we're in a stressful situation, we think a moment before we react impulsively, responding with patience and compassion instead of anger. We try to be kind and helpful, and refrain from hurtful, self-interested, negative actions and faultfinding.

Applying spiritual practice in daily life begins when you wake up in the morning. Rejoice that you didn't die in the night, knowing you have one more useful day—you can't guarantee that you'll have two. Then remind yourself of correct motivation. Instead of setting out to become rich and famous or to follow your own selfish interests, meet the day with an altruistic intention to help others. And renew your commitment every morning. Tell yourself, "With this day I'll do the very best that I can. In the past I've done fairly well on some days, terribly on others. But since this day may be my last, I will offer my very best; I will do right by other people as much as I am able."

Before you go to sleep at night, don't just hit the pillow and pass out. Instead, review the day. Ask yourself, "How did I do? I had the intention not to hurt anybody—did I accomplish that? I meant to cultivate joy, compassion, love, equanimity—did I do so?" Think not just of this day, but of every day of your life. "Have I developed positive tendencies? Have I been basically a virtuous person? Or have I spent most of my time acting negatively, engaged in nonvirtuous activities?" Ask yourself these things critically and honestly. How does it come out when you really study the tallies?

If you find that you have fallen short, there's no benefit in feeling guilty or blaming yourself. The point is to observe what you have done, because your harmful actions can be purified. Negativity is not marked indelibly in the ground of the mind. It can be changed. So look back. When you see your faults and downfalls, call upon a wisdom being. You don't need to go to a special place, for there is no place where prayer is not heard. It doesn't matter if you consider perfection to be God, Buddha, or a deity, as long as when you objectify it, there is no flaw, no fault, no limitation. From absolute perfection you gain the blessings of purification.

Confess, with that wisdom being as your witness, and sincerely regret the harm you've done, vowing not to repeat it. As you meditate, visualize light radiating from the object of perfection, cleansing you and purifying all the mistakes of your day, your life, every life you've lived.

When you look at your day, you may find that you were able to make others happy. Maybe you gave food to a hungry animal or practiced generosity, patience. Rather than becoming self-satisfied, resolve to do better tomorrow, to be more skillful, more compassionate in your interactions with others. Dedicate the positive energy created by your actions to all beings, whoever they are, whatever condition they're in, thinking, "May this virtue relieve the suffering of beings; may it cause them short- and long-term happiness."

During the day, check your mind. How am I behaving? What is my real intention? You can't really know anybody else's mind; the only one you truly know is your own. Whenever you can, contemplate these thoughts: the preciousness of human birth, impermanence, karma, the suffering of others.

In daily meditation practice we work with two aspects of the mind: its capacity to reason and conceptualize—the intellect—and the quality that is beyond thought—the pervasive, nonconceptual nature of mind. Using the rational faculty, contemplate. Then let the mind rest. Think and then relax; contemplate, then relax. Don't use one or the other exclusively, but both together, like the two wings of a bird.

This isn't something you do only sitting on a cushion. You can meditate this way anywhere—while driving your car, while working. It doesn't require special props or a special environment. It can be practiced in all walks of life.

Some people think that if they meditate for fifteen minutes a day, they ought to become enlightened in a week and a half. But it doesn't work like that. Even if you meditate and pray and contemplate for an hour of the day, that's one hour you're meditating and twenty-three you're not. What are the chances of one person against twenty-three in a tug-of-war? One pulls one way, twenty-three the other—who's going to win?

It's not possible to change the mind with one hour of daily meditation. You have to pay attention to your spiritual process throughout the day, as you work, play, sleep; the mind always has to be moving toward the ultimate goal of enlightenment.

When you are out and about in the world, keep your mind with what you are doing. If you are writing, keep your mind on the pen. If you are sewing, focus your mind on the stitch. Don't get distracted. Don't think of a hundred things at the same time. Don't get going on what happened yesterday or what might happen in the future. It doesn't matter what the work is if you focus the mind and stay with what you undertake. Hold to it closely, comfortable in what you do, and in that way you will train the mind.

Always check yourself thoroughly, reduce negative thoughts, speech, and behavior, increase those that are positive. Think carefully, and continually refocus, because you can get blurry very easily. What meditation produces is a constant refocusing. You have to bring pure intention back again and again. And then relax the mind, to allow a direct, subtle recognition of that which lies beyond all thought.

There are, of course, established centers where you can hear the teachings of the Buddha, places where you are exposed to a different worldview, where you can meditate and contemplate in an environment in which others are doing likewise. It's hard to make progress on your own, hard to change if you hear the teachings only once. It's very helpful to visit such centers, but whether you can or not, you need to sew the patch on your clothes with a care that requires constant attention, hearing and applying the teachings again and again.

It doesn't happen swiftly, but the mind can change. There was once a man in India who decided to measure his thoughts. This wasn't easy, for though one can be determined to watch one's thoughts, many get away, those not seen as they pass by, that come and go without our awareness. Nevertheless, he put down a white stone for every virtuous thought, a black stone for every nonvirtuous one. At first this produced a huge pile of black stones, but very slowly, as the years went by, the pile of black stones became smaller and the white pile grew. That's the kind of gradual progress we make with sincere effort. There's noth-

ing flashy about the progress of the mind; it's very mea-
sured and steady, requiring diligence, attentiveness, patience, and enthusiastic perseverance.

In the tradition of Buddhism there are many profound
teachings, but what we've been discussing is the essential
sweet nectar of them all. Cultivating good heart throughout
daily life, practicing virtue, compassion, equanimity, love,
and joy—this is the way to enlightenment.

Part II

*The Four Thoughts That
Turn the Mind*

6   The Importance of the Four Thoughts

From the biographies of great practitioners, we see that exemplary saints and masters were unflagging in their pursuit of the spiritual path. They were willing to put up with all manner of challenges and hardships, practicing day and night with inspiration and enthusiasm, because their understanding and assimilation of the contemplations known in Buddhism as "the four thoughts that turn the mind toward dharma" were so profound.

Contemplation of the four thoughts upholds our practice, just as a foundation sustains a building. In constructing a home, if we arrange the foundational stones so that they hold firmly and don't shift, we can build a fine structure, one we can live in for a very long time. If, instead, we take whatever comes to hand and throw something up overnight, we won't end up with anything useful. Sooner or later the whole construction will come tumbling down.

Similarly, if we listen to, contemplate, and practice the dharma, the teachings of the Buddha, only superficially, we may discover after ten or fifteen years that there's been no real change, that we experience the same desire and attachment, ignorance, anger, and aggression as before. Bound by ordinary habits of mind, we find our capacity to benefit ourselves and others severely limited. We might be tempted to conclude that there is something wrong with the teachings, that Buddhist methods don't work. But they work just fine; it's the practitioner who won't work, who isn't making the necessary effort to change.

We must strive from the depth of our hearts to develop a firm foundation for our practice. Otherwise, we'll easily fault the teachings and become discouraged. We'll fabricate all kinds of excuses to avoid practicing; all sorts of outer circumstances and inner obstacles—disease, physical discomfort, mental stress—will seem to stand in the way.

Among the obstacles to our path is the fact that we're dominated by our attachments. We have many needs and desires we feel we absolutely must fulfill. By meditating on two of the four thoughts—first, the freedom and opportunity of our precious human existence and the difficulty of obtaining it, and second, impermanence—we come to realize that our precious human birth is as rare as our time is short. These two contemplations help to reduce the mind's poisons and steer us toward liberation. Carrying these thoughts with us throughout our daily lives—with our families, at work, or in formal meditation—we develop more equanimity and ease in dealing with life's changes. In reordering our priorities, we develop contentment as well, for we come to understand that enough is enough—when we have a hundred of something, we don't need a thousand; when we have ten thousand, we don't need a million—that if we continually try to satisfy ever-increasing worldly demands and desires, we will always remain discontented.

Nonetheless, we may still find ourselves seeking only relative rather than ultimate happiness, thinking only of how to make our worldly circumstances the very best they can be in this and future lives. Because such shortsightedness creates further obstacles to liberation, we meditate on the second two of the four thoughts—the karmic process of cause and effect, and the suffering that pervades cyclic existence. Through these two contemplations, we reduce our attachment to conventional happiness and experience a gradual loosening of ever more subtle ties to samsara.

With less attachment to our worldly experience, we turn toward the path to enlightenment, removing everything counterproductive, bringing together everything supportive to our goal. This is why the four thoughts are called the preliminaries. If we want a cart to take us someplace, we must put a horse before that cart.

Many people believe these teachings are for beginners. They want to hurry on to something "profound," beyond what they think of as "kindergarten dharma." But the contemplation of the four thoughts is among the most profound and beneficial practices on the path to enlightenment. For these are the foundational truths that underlie the entire spiritual path.

7 The Lama

Contemplation of the four thoughts is among the skillful methods we use to reduce the mind's poisons and create short- and long-term benefit for ourselves and others. Since we don't have the fortune to have met and learned the methods of liberation directly from the Buddha Shakyamuni, it is the lama, our spiritual teacher, who introduces such teachings to us. Yet before we come to rely on a spiritual teacher, it is essential that we carefully research that teacher's qualities, just as we would investigate a doctor's qualifications before placing our life in that person's hands. In a sense, if we didn't investigate a doctor, it wouldn't be such a big deal, because mistreatment might cause us to lose only this one life. But if we place our faith in a spiritual teacher who isn't qualified, we might develop counterproductive habits that could remain with us for lifetimes to come and create tremendous obstacles on the path to enlightenment.

Two qualities are necessary in a teacher: first, that he or she has listened to, contemplated, and understood the teachings and, second, has meditated upon them and gained realization of their essential meaning. Eloquence is not the most important quality of a dharma teacher, for it's not so difficult to deliver a nice lecture; what's crucial is that, through a genuine and profound practice of medi-

46

tation, he or she maintains a direct, personal experience of the teachings. Otherwise, the teacher might be like a parrot who repeats again and again, "Practice virtue, don't practice nonvirtue" but who devours an insect as soon as it enters the cage.

These days it's difficult to check a teacher's qualities. At least one out of every ten or twenty people claims to be a teacher with great scholarly and meditational achievement. No one hangs out a shingle declaring "I am a bad teacher." Ideally one should discover from an outside source how and where a teacher studied the dharma and practiced meditation. But it is even more important to observe the teacher firsthand, to check carefully whether he or she has good heart and truly lives the teachings. It would be hard to find a completely faultless teacher—and even if we did, we wouldn't realize it. Nonetheless, we can rely on a lama who, through meditation practice, has removed some of the mind's obscurations, attained some degree of realization, and developed great compassion. Teachers with good heart have your interests, not theirs, in mind. If they can't answer a question or help you, they will direct you to someone who can. They won't lead you astray.

It's risky to make too hasty a commitment to a teacher. But once you have come to a carefully considered decision, you must follow his or her teachings diligently and purposefully. To use the example of a doctor again, if you are sick but don't take the medication your physician prescribes, you won't get well. So after looking for a teacher skillfully, you must listen and train skillfully. If you carefully apply the instructions you've received, then slowly, your negativity will decrease and love and compassion will increase. In this way, you will learn what the teacher has learned. The teacher is like a mold that shapes the student's mind. A student won't develop good qualities from a poor teacher, but will benefit infallibly by following a good teacher's instructions.

This is why, at the beginning of our contemplation of the four thoughts, we call upon the lama. We remember the lama's qualities and pray that through the lama's blessings obstacles to our practice will dissolve, our mind will turn toward the dharma, and the door to liberation will be opened.

8 *The First Foundational Thought: Precious Human Birth*

Imagine that you are very poor and suddenly find yourself in a land where everything is studded with gems, gold, and coins. You live there for many years, but one day must return home, making a perilous journey by sea, with no possibility of ever returning to the jeweled land. Once home, you realize you hadn't thought to bring anything with you, not a single jewel, not a speck of gold dust, nothing; think how regretful you would be.

In the same way, we move lifetime after lifetime through the cycles of suffering, lacking the merit—the virtue and positive energy—necessary to propel us out of samsara. Then a few rare conditions come together to produce this precious human existence with its immense opportunity. If we die without using it to full advantage, we will have left the human realm empty-handed, having accomplished nothing. The first thought that turns the mind toward dharma concerns the preciousness of our human birth and the importance of using it well.

People sometimes wonder, "Why was I born? What is the purpose of this human life? I have a feeling there is some great reason for my being here, but I don't know what it is." Some think their purpose is to be a fine musician or to write outstanding books. Yet any music played, anything written is impermanent.

We don't understand that our mind is the dreamer and our life experience the dream it has made. Because we have no idea that we are dreaming, we take life very seriously and often feel helpless when things don't go as we wish. Through spiritual practice, at the very least we can make happy dreams. Eventually, we can actually wake up.

Waking up, revealing the essence of our existence, is the overriding purpose of our lives. But what is this essence? It can't be our body, since all that is left when our mind leaves the body is a corpse. Nor can it be the speech faculty, since that is simply a function of the body. And it isn't the superficial vacillations of the emotions, either, the continuous up and down of hope and fear, liking and disliking, or the activity of mind that, like a jumping flea or popping corn, is always moving and changing. To find the essence, we have to realize the true nature of our body, speech, and mind, beyond our dreamlike experience of reality. The capacity to do so can be found only in the precious human birth.

We cannot assume that, having been human once, we'll be guaranteed a human existence again and again. A human body is very difficult to obtain. It requires the accumulation of a vast amount of merit through scrupulously pure discipline in past lifetimes. Discipline of this kind involves three things: not performing negative acts or harmful behavior; cultivating virtuous thoughts and actions; and having as one's motivation for observing the first two disciplines an altruistic desire to benefit others. It is only because we have amassed this amount of merit, coupled with the aspiration to be reborn as a human being, that we are here now, in the human realm.

Precious human birth provides a freedom and leisure to practice that cannot be found in other realms of experience, either the three lower realms—the hell, hungry ghost, and animal realms—with their immense suffering, or the nonhuman higher realms—the worldly god and jealous god, or demigod, realms—with their false contentment.

When we say "precious human birth" we are not referring to nominal human existence, in which one is born, lives, dies, and then one's consciousness goes on to some other experience. A human rebirth is precious only when endowed with eight types of leisure and ten qualities and conditions.

The three lower realms allow no opportunity to hear or understand the teachings of dharma. Beings there lack leisure or other supportive circumstances to aide or encourage practice: they experience too much suffering.

On the other hand, the god realms provide no incentive to practice. Beings in these realms are so infatuated with and intoxicated by sensual pleasures and bliss that the thought of escaping from this or any other state of cyclic existence never occurs to them.

In these realms, there is neither the incentive nor opportunity to seek liberation from the cycles of samsaric suffering. In the human realm, however, we taste both sweet and sour. We know enough about suffering to want change, yet the suffering isn't so acute that we can't do anything about it.

Nonetheless, there are four types of human existence that lack sufficient leisure for practice. First, one might be born in a culture dominated by wrong view—the idea that killing or harming others is virtuous or spiritual, for example. Second, one might be born skeptical about spirituality and religion. Mere intellectual sophistication or scholarly learning doesn't enable one to acquire or maintain spiritual faith. Clever but cynical people find it difficult to put their trust in anything and thus don't have the openness and receptivity necessary to look for a spiritual practice. Third, one might be born in a dark aeon—an era in which no buddha manifests in any form in the human realm to offer Buddhist or other beneficial spiritual teachings. Finally, one might be afflicted with a physical or mental handicap that makes it impossible to listen to or understand the teachings.

We need to realize the tremendous advantage we enjoy, having not been born in any of these situations. Our precious human birth provides us with enormous freedom to practice. It also endows us with ten special qualities and conditions, five of which accrue from who we are and five from outer circumstances.

The first five qualities include our human body itself, which can be a vehicle to enlightenment; our birth in an area where the teachings are available rather than in a "border country," one where the influence of the dharma or other pure spiritual teachings has not spread; the fact that our faculties are intact and our intelligence sufficient for us to understand the teachings; a karmic predisposition to develop spiritually rather than waste this opportunity or use our life to harm others; and a receptivity to the Buddhist path or other spiritual traditions that offer short- and long-term benefit for ourselves and others.

The first of the five conditions deriving from our outer circumstances is that a buddha has indeed appeared. Were we born into a universe where no buddha had ever manifested, the question of liberation wouldn't even come up because we would have no historical example. By attaining enlightenment in our realm and demonstrating that it can be done, the Buddha Shakyamuni offered us an extraordinary opportunity.

The second condition is that, having appeared, the Buddha taught dharma. Even though we might have the historical example of the Buddha, without his teachings there would be no route to follow.

The tradition of teachings that has been preserved and passed on throughout history comprises the third condition. Again, a buddha may appear and teach during a given generation, and beings may benefit, but the teachings might be lost or gradually die out. In our case, the teachings of Buddhism have endured to this day.

The fourth condition arises from the presence of practitioners who have realized, and provide a living transmission of, the teachings. Through their example, the teachings become accessible to us.

Finally, due to the kindness and compassion of the lama, his or her willingness to teach and become involved with others rather than practice in solitude, we ourselves can learn, practice, and accomplish the teachings.

If we didn't enjoy all of these eighteen leisures and conditions, we couldn't even talk about the first of the four thoughts. We could never fulfill the true purpose of our precious human existence, never attain the goal of dispelling suffering and bringing about happiness for ourselves and others in both a temporary and an ultimate sense.

By contemplating over and over again the value of our precious human existence we come to see that this birth is better than a wish-fulfilling gem. There are many stories of those who go to immense trouble, traveling long distances, enduring all kinds of hardships and life-threatening situations, to acquire such a gem; and yet at the end of their search what have they accomplished? The gem's magic may make them wealthy for a while, or find them an enchanting mate, or manifest a big home. But these things last only a certain amount of time. The gem can't produce enlightenment. With the skillful use of our human existence, not only can we realize short-term benefits, we can achieve liberation from samsara and acquire the capacity to help others do so as well.

The rarity of our human existence becomes very clear when we compare the number of beings in the human realm with the number of those in the other five realms. Traditionally, it is said that hell beings are as countless as the dust particles in the entire universe. The hungry ghosts, slightly fewer in number, are said to be as numerous as the grains of sand in the river Ganges. As to animal life, there is no corner of land or drop of the ocean that isn't teeming with it—just as a container for making alcohol brims with grain. The number of beings in the demigod realm can be compared to the number of snowflakes in a blizzard, the number of beings in the human and worldly god realms to the number of dust particles on the surface of a thumbnail. Those endowed with a precious human birth, the exalted aspiration to free all beings from suffering, are as rare as stars in the noonday sky.

The Buddha illustrated the rarity of the precious human birth with a metaphor comparing the entire three-thousand-fold universe to a huge ocean with a wooden yoke floating somewhere on top of it. The yoke is continually buffeted by the wind, the waves, and the currents. At the bottom of the ocean lives a blind turtle. Once every hundred years it comes to the surface for a gulp of air, then goes back down to the bottom. The laws of chance are such that, sooner or later, the moment the turtle surfaces the wind will blow the yoke over its head and the turtle will poke through. That this will happen is just barely conceivable. According to the Buddha, the chances of someone finding a precious human birth are even less likely.

Once we appreciate the rarity of our precious human birth and the opportunity it provides us, we begin to under-stand that we shouldn't waste it but rather should fulfill its deeper purpose—to reveal the essence of our existence, the true nature of mind.

9 The Second Foundational Thought: Impermanence

One of the best methods for developing pure spiritual practice is to meditate continually on impermanence. We begin by looking at the inanimate universe. At some point aeons ago, there was nothing substantial here. In the Buddhist cosmology, the element of wind first appeared, giving rise to the elements of fire, then water and earth, as the physical universe came into being, with Mount Meru in the center surrounded by the four continents. Then life forms began to arise, first from cellular division, then from various kinds of asexual reproduction, and then sexual reproduction, including egg and womb birth.

This vast period of creation culminated in the present "era of duration," during which there will be eighteen cycles of increasing and decreasing well-being and happiness. As the universe nears its end and the physical environment is no longer conducive to life, more and more beings will be reborn in other universes. Finally, physical matter will disintegrate until, once again, none of it remains.

As we think about these things, our perception of the universe will start to change. We'll realize that no matter how true and reliable it may seem, it is not eternal. On a smaller scale, we'll see that mountain ranges have come and gone, and where huge oceans surged, there now stands dry land. Where towns once flourished, empty wasteland exists today, and on former wasteland, huge cities have grown up. We will become conscious of continual change in our environment, from prehistoric time through recorded history.

Change is continuous. Day by day one season slips into the next. Day turns to night and night to day. Buildings don't suddenly grow old; rather, second by second, from the moment they're constructed, they begin to deteriorate.

Our environment, physical body, speech, and thoughts change as swiftly as a needle piercing a rose petal. If you pierce a pile of cupped rose petals with a needle, it may seem to be a single movement, but it actually consists of many discrete steps. You penetrate each petal separately, going through its outside edge, through the middle, out the other side, through the space between that petal and the next, through one side of the next, and so on. The increment of time it takes the needle to pass through each of those successive stages can be used as a unit of measure to describe the rate of change of all phenomena in our world.

Think of the beings inhabiting this universe. How many people born a hundred years ago are still alive? How many of us now on this earth will be here a hundred years from today? Historic figures—no matter how rich they were, how famous, how successful, how much territory they controlled—are now only legends. A story is often told in the Buddhist teachings of a king so powerful he controlled not only the known world but the realm of Indra, king of the gods. Yet only his legend remains.

Extraordinary masters of the past—the eight great dharma kings, the twenty-five principal disciples of the great teacher Padmasambhava, even the Buddha Shakyamuni, a manifestation of supreme compassion in human form, who was born in a grove in Lumbini (now Nepal) and throughout his life performed twelve great deeds—are no longer here. This doesn't mean that their blessings died with their physical bodies, for the positive qualities of enlightened mind pervade the three times of past, present, and future. But from our individual perspective, they have disappeared, just as when the world turns it appears to us that the sun has set.

We see the play of impermanence in our relationships as well. How many of our family members, friends, people in our hometown have died? How many have moved away, disappearing from our lives forever?

As little children, we couldn't bear to be away from our parents. Sometimes, when our mother left the room for two or three minutes, we panicked. Now we write to our parents maybe once a year. Perhaps they live on the other side of the world. We might not even know whether they're alive. How things have changed!

At one time we felt happy just being near a person we loved. Just to hold that person's hand made us feel wonderful. Now maybe we can't stand him, we don't want to know anything about him. Whatever comes together must fall apart, whatever once gathered must separate, whatever was born must die. Continual change, relentless change is constant in our world.

"So," you might think, "the universe continuously changes, and likewise relationships, yet 'I' am always the same." But what is "I"? Is it the body? Upon conception, the human body begins as a single cell, then multiplies into a cell mass that differentiates into various organ systems. After coming into the world a fully formed infant, we begin to grow moment by moment into an adult.

This physical process takes place week by week, month by month, until eventually we realize that things are getting a little worse rather than a little better. We are no longer growing up; we are aging. Inexorably, we lose certain capacities: our eyesight fails, our hearing dims, our thinking processes become muddled. This is impermanence taking its toll.

If we live a normal life span and die a natural death, we'll become more and more feeble, until one day we won't be able to get out of bed. Perhaps we won't be able to feed ourselves, eliminate, or recognize those around us. At a certain point, we'll die, our body an empty shell, our mind wandering in the after-death experience. This body, which was so important for so long, will be burned or buried. It might even be devoured by wild animals or birds. At a certain point nothing will remain to remind anyone of our ever having been here. We'll become nothing more than a memory.

"Well," you might think, "the body is impermanent, but the 'real me,' my mind, is not." However, if you look at your mind, you'll see that it isn't the same as it was when you were an infant. Then, all you wanted was your mother's milk and a warm place to sleep. A little later, a few toys made you happy. Later it was a girlfriend or boyfriend, and later a certain job or marriage or home. Your needs, desires, and values have changed, not all at once, but second by second. Even within each day, the mind experiences happiness and sadness, virtuous and nonvirtuous thoughts, many times over. If we try to grasp one particular moment, even as we think to grasp it, it disappears.

Like the body and mind, our speech is constantly changing: every word we utter is lost, another rushing to replace it. There is nothing we can point to as unchanging, stable, permanent.

We must instill in ourselves an ongoing, moment-by-moment awareness of impermanence. For life is a race against death and the time of death unknown. Contemplating the approach of death changes our priorities and helps us let go of our obsession with ordinary involvements. If we always remain aware that each moment might be our last, we will intensify our practice in order not to waste or misuse our precious human opportunity. As our contemplation of this truth matures, it will be easy to grasp the highest, most profound Buddhist teachings. We will have some comprehension of how the world works, how appearances arise and change. We will move from a mere intellectual understanding of impermanence to the realization that everything we have based our belief of reality upon is just a shimmering radiance of change. We will begin to see that everything is illusory, like a dream or mirage. Though phenomena appear, in truth nothing stable is really there.

Then what, we might ask, will be of benefit to us when we die? It doesn't matter how pleasant or congenial people now think we are; after we're dead they won't want our body around. Nor will they be able to go with us, no matter who they are or how happy they've made us. We have to die alone. That is true, even if we are famous, even if we are as wealthy as the god of wealth himself. At the time of death, all the wealth we have accumulated, all the power, status, and fame we have achieved, all the friends we have gathered—none of these will be of any help to us. Our consciousness will be plucked from our surroundings as cleanly as a hair from butter. The only thing that will benefit us is our practice of the dharma; the only thing that will follow us at death, our positive and negative karma. Nothing else.

Question: If we contemplate impermanence like this, won't we become apathetic to the needs of others?
Response: Our intention on the dharma path is to relieve the suffering of others as much as we can, in every way we can,

until ultimately we are able to relieve all beings of all suffering. At the same time, we maintain an awareness of impermanence in everything we do, remembering that, like a dream, everyday life occurs but isn't inherently true. We do all we can in the context of this dream experience to benefit others and to reduce the mind's poisons so that we won't cause ourselves and others harm. If we practice virtue and reduce nonvirtue, this dream we call life will get better. Remembering the dreamlike and impermanent nature of our experience, we will eventually wake up and help others to do so as well.

As our realization of impermanence and the illusory nature of reality increases, so does our compassion. We see that, trapped by their belief in the dream, having no understanding of impermanence, beings suffer tremendous anguish. Because they believe in the solidity of their experience, they react to their arising karma with attachment and aversion, making more negative karma and perpetuating the cycles of suffering.

Question: What's the difference between contemplating impermanence and looking at your watch, wondering how soon whatever you're doing will be finished?

Response: It comes down to motivation. If your motivation is selfless, you won't notice the clock much. If it isn't, then things will seem to take longer than you'd expect. I wouldn't discourage you from clock watching, but watch samsara's clock: ask yourself how soon samsara will be finished. Then the question becomes, "How can I cut attachment? How can I cut aversion? How can I cut confusion?" By eliminating the mind's obscurations, we can eventually bring samsara to an end.

Question: I think what you're saying is true, but I still find that the weight of my many years of not thinking this way is stronger than my belief in the teaching on impermanence. How can I change that habit?

Response: Suppose we start with a very simple exercise. Examine the importance you place on the food you eat, your clothes, your house, your friends, your conversations, the books you read. You'll probably find that you hold them to be so crucial you work night and day to maintain them.

Now examine these things differently. Look at each in turn and ask yourself whether it is permanent. Ask yourself whether it is something you can ultimately depend upon. At the hour of your death and beyond, will it be reliable? And is it worth all the effort and concern that you devote to it now? Thinking about impermanence and death helps to cut through worldly values and changes your priorities.

Through contemplation and application of the teachings in each moment of your life, you will see your habits change. You won't change only by reading books. You must search and probe, question and examine. You may have already been exposed to all kinds of ideas and understood many things intellectually, but without contemplation that takes you deeper in your practice and allows you to reach some very fundamental conclusions, you won't be able to make the next step.

To discover what's really important to you, you could take a few minutes now to reflect on what's been said here and see how it relates to your own experience. Only through contemplation will you find out whether spiritual practice has heart and meaning for you.

10 The Third Foundational Thought: Karma

Although some people think the principle of karma exists only in Buddhist doctrine, it can actually be found in almost all spiritual traditions. It is usually stated simply: "If you're good, you'll go to heaven, you'll be happy. If you're bad, you'll go to hell, you'll suffer." In these traditions, the principle of inevitable consequence we call karma is like a train with only two destinations, heaven and hell. The Buddhist view is that the train has many stops in between. The greater one's goodness, the greater one's experience of happiness. The greater one's negativity, the greater one's suffering and pain. Our present everyday reality is the karmic outcome of our thoughts, words, and deeds in this and former lifetimes.

Some people have difficulty with Buddhism's more extensive view of karma because they don't believe in reincarnation. Since they can't verify that they or anyone else will have a future existence or that they've had any previous ones, they can't accept the idea of rebirth. But the fact that we can't remember past lives or glimpse future ones is not a sufficient reason for not believing in them. There are many things we have confidence in though we can't see or empirically verify them. Like tomorrow! We can't prove that tomorrow is going to happen, but we're willing to bet that it will. People can't prove that at a certain age they're going to retire, live off whatever they've set aside, relax and have a good time, yet many are saving for that. In the same way, the inability to remember or foresee other lifetimes doesn't mean they don't exist.

Karma can be likened to a seed, which, under the proper conditions, will yield a plant. If you sow a barley seed, you can be certain you'll get a barley shoot. The seed won't come up rice.

The mind is like a fertile field—all sorts of things can grow there. When we plant a seed—an act, a statement, or a thought—it will eventually produce a fruit, which will ripen and fall to the ground and perpetuate more of the same. Moment by moment, we plant potent seeds of causation with our body, speech, and mind. When the right conditions come together for our karma to ripen, we will have to deal with the consequences of what we have planted.

Although we are responsible for what we sow, we forget that we've planted these seeds, and either give credit to or blame people or things outside of us when they ripen. We're like a bird perched on a rock who can see its shadow but, when it flies away, forgets that the shadow exists. Each time it lands, the bird thinks it's found a completely different shadow. In the moment, we have a thought, we speak or act. But we lose sight of the fact that each thought, word, and action will produce a result. When the fruit finally ripens, we think, "Why did this happen to me? I've done nothing to deserve this."

Once we have committed a negative action, unless it is purified we will experience its consequences. We can't shirk the responsibility or try to make the karma disappear by justifying it. It doesn't work that way. Whoever commits an act will infallibly experience its results, whether positive or negative.

Every movement of our thoughts, words, and deeds is like a stitch in the fabric of our coming reality. Latent in our present experience are oceans of karma from countless past lifetimes, which under the proper conditions will come to fruition.

In order to find liberation from samsara, we must work at the causal level, not the level of results, the pleasure and pain that are the consequences of our behavior. To do so, we need to purify our earlier mistakes and change the mind that plants the seeds of suffering, purify the mental poisons that perpetuate endless karma. This process is called "closing the door of nonvirtue," averting karmic consequences by taking preventive measures, no longer acting upon the faults of the mind.

We speak of positive, negative, and neutral karma. Acts that generate positive karma lead to personal happiness and happiness for others. Negative karma brings about suffering for ourselves and others. When our intention is to benefit others, we create virtuous thoughts, speech, and actions and positive karma. When we are motivated by the mind's poisons, we create nonvirtuous thoughts, speech, and actions and negative karma.

Neutral karma is generated by innocuous actions, actions motivated neither by the desire to harm nor by the intention to help. Because it has no positive effect, it is considered to be nonvirtuous. That is why karma is often discussed as only positive or negative.

Altruistic motivation can lead to either exhaustible or inexhaustible positive karma. We create exhaustible karma when our motivation is to benefit others but our frame of reference remains short term. For example, we might feed a hungry person or nurse someone sick, but our goal remains temporary, not one of helping that person and all other beings awaken from the cycles of suffering. Consequently, the happiness that results from our virtuous action is temporary and will end when the good karma we've created by that action becomes exhausted. It won't lead to liberation from samsara.

When an action is undertaken with the intention that a particular person, as well as all other beings, not only find temporary happiness but awaken from cyclic existence, it produces inexhaustible positive karma. Such karma results not only in happiness in the higher realms of experience, but ultimately in enlightenment.

We need to become absolutely certain of the infallibility of the karmic process constantly at work in our lives, for our endless suffering, our experiences of higher and lower states of rebirth, are rooted in the inexorable working out of good and bad karma.

There was once a hermit who lived and meditated in a forest. He had only one set of clothes, which he usually washed in a stream, and over time, they began to fade. One day he decided to restore their original color, heated a pot of dye, and placed the clothing in it.

Meanwhile, a farmer was searching the area for a lost calf. He saw the smoke from the hermit's fire and immediately assumed that somebody had stolen and slaughtered his calf and was cooking it. He came to the clearing and, finding no one around, looked into the pot. There he saw the head and limbs of the calf boiling in the water. He ran to the king, crying, "This man claiming to be a great sage is nothing but a common thief. He stole my calf and is busy cooking it for his dinner right now." The king was outraged because this spiritual person who had been living in his domain, gathering students, teaching, and gaining fame and respect had turned out to be a thief. He sent his soldiers to arrest the hermit and throw him in prison.

Actually, the calf had only wandered off, and after seven days found its way back to the farmer, alive and well. Very contrite, the farmer went straight to the king and confessed, "This is terrible! I've slandered this great saint. Please let him out of prison immediately." The king agreed to do so but, being very busy, forgot all about it.

Seven months later, the sage was still in jail. Finally, one of his students, who possessed great meditative powers, flew through the air to the king and said, "My teacher has done nothing wrong. Please let him go!"

The king instantly remembered and went to the dungeon himself to release the sage. He was overcome with remorse not only for having arrested him without due process but for having forgotten to let him out.

The hermit told the king, "You've nothing to be sorry for. This was my karma. In a previous lifetime I stole and killed a calf. As I was running away from the owner, I came across a holy person meditating in the forest. I thought I would place the blame on him by dumping the carcass outside his hut and running away. He was wrongly accused and thrown in prison for seven days. The consequences of that action were so negative that my mindstream underwent rebirth after rebirth in lower realms of existence. Now, having attained this human life, I have been able to continue my spiritual development. But some residual karma had to be purified. From my point of view, things have turned out very well."

It's crucial that we understand what is virtuous and nonvirtuous. Otherwise, even as practitioners trying to be of greater benefit, we may actually create more harm than good. The subtle flaw of pride might arise: "I'm such a spiritual person," or "My tradition is the best one," or "Those poor folks who don't have a spiritual path!" When we make such judgments, we only produce negative karma. If we fail to use our body and mind in a careful, disciplined way, our flaws can worsen. Our minds are rife with the five poisons. With these paints in our palette, what kind of picture will we create?

We produce physical nonvirtue through killing, stealing, or sexual misconduct. A fully nonvirtuous action has four parts. For example, the act of killing includes identifying the object to be killed; establishing the motivation to kill; committing the act of killing; and finally the fact of the victim's death. If we have the intention to kill someone but don't carry through with it, we still generate half the non-virtue by identifying the object and establishing the motivation to kill. Or if in walking down the sidewalk we accidentally step on an ant and kill it, we also create half the nonvirtue of killing.

Stealing means taking something that hasn't been given to you. It includes taking something without the owner knowing it, overpowering a person in order to appropriate something, or using a position of power or authority to seize something from another in order to benefit oneself.

Sexual misconduct involves sexual activity with someone underage, with someone who is sick, or when such activity will cause mental or emotional distress or the breaking of one's own or another's vows or commitment to a sexual partner.

The four nonvirtues of speech include lying, the worst lie being that of falsely claiming that one has spiritual realization; slander, which involves using speech to separate close friends, the worst case being that of slandering members of one's spiritual group; harsh speech that hurts others; and gossip or useless speech, which wastes one's own and others' time.

The first of the three nonvirtues of the mind is covetousness. The second nonvirtue consists of harmful thoughts: wanting to harm another, wishing that another might be harmed, or rejoicing in harm done to another.

The third mental nonvirtue is wrong view. Having wrong view means thinking in very contrary ways, as opposed to doubting and questioning, which is a healthy component of spiritual contemplation. Believing that it's good to be bad, or bad to be good is an example of wrong view. So is disbelieving in the illusory nature of experience because we can't prove it and thus denying the basic truth that will ultimately produce liberation from suffering. For although we may not be able to prove that our experience is illusory, neither can we prove that it isn't.

The ten virtues follow clearly from the ten nonvirtues. Saving and protecting life, for example, creates tremendous virtue. All beings are equal in that they all seek happiness, don't want to suffer, and value their lives as much as we do. To save the life of an insect or an animal is extremely virtuous and, when the merit is dedicated, creates great benefit not only for that animal but for all beings. Merit dedicated to the long life of others, for example, can be of immense benefit to those who are sick.

Generosity, no matter how seemingly insignificant—even giving a bit of food or water to a hungry bird—produces great virtue. Maintaining discipline in sexual relationships, telling the truth, using speech to create harmony, to help another's mind, and to create temporary and ultimate benefit for oneself and others—these, too, are virtues, as are rejoicing in the happiness of others, generating helpful and kind thoughts, and learning correct view.

The karmic fruit of a nonvirtuous action is similar whether you yourself perform the action, ask someone else to do so, or rejoice when others accomplish it. If you recite one hundred mantras alone, you create the virtue of reciting that number of mantras. But if a group of ten people recite one hundred mantras, each member of that group generates the virtue of reciting a thousand mantras. Similarly, if a person in a group kills someone, each member of the group generates the same nonvirtue.

Although it may appear that our situation is hopeless, through confession and purification we can avert the negative karma we have accumulated from beginningless time. It's said that the only virtue of nonvirtue is that it can be purified.

When I was a little boy, a woman came to visit my mother. She wore a necklace with a flat, luminous object dangling from it. Fascinated, I asked her what it was.

"A fish bone," she replied.

I wanted it! I had to have one like it! So I ran to the river and caught a small fish, thinking it must have a beautiful bone inside. I put the fish down and took out my knife. I couldn't stand to look as I tried to cut the fish, so I turned my face away. But my knife was dull and I couldn't make the fish die. It just flopped around and finally died from exposure to the air. When it stopped moving, I cut it open and looked inside. There was no bone like the one the woman wore around her neck.

Chagrined, I returned home and told the lady, "I looked inside a fish, but I couldn't find a bone like this."

"No, no, no," she said. "You can only find such a bone in fishes that live in the big ocean."

It was then that I realized maybe I had done something wrong. I had killed a fish and it wasn't even the right kind.

Later, when I was twenty-two years old and in my second three-year meditation retreat, I had a dream in which I gazed out over a huge expanse of water. The sky and the water met. I'd never seen anything like that in landlocked Tibet, not even in a picture. I asked, "What is this?" Someone in the dream said, "This is where you will be reborn." Then I remembered the fish and realized that this was the karma I had created by killing it. I prayed, "If I'm going to be reborn a fish, let me be a little fish so that I won't make more bad karma by eating other fish."

When I awoke very early the next morning, a fish appeared in the dark in front of me. Everywhere I turned, the fish was there. I couldn't get away from it. I began to recite the mantra *Om Mani Padme Hung* in the breaks between my retreat practice sessions, dedicating the virtue of my practice to the fish I'd killed. After I had finished a million recitations, the fish finally disappeared. I think now I may have purified my fish karma.

We don't need to know exactly what karma we are purifying to apply a particular method; purification techniques address all manner of negative karma. The development of compassion and loving kindness, selflessness, meditation on and prayer to enlightened beings, the recitation of mantra—all of these help to diminish our present suffering, to make us more careful in our practice of harmlessness, and to purify the causes of future suffering.

However, if while doing purification practice we think, "I have so much bad karma to purify" or "I really want to attain buddhahood," our motivation isn't pure. This kind of self-interested practice is less effective than generating pure compassion outside of formal practice. The most effective approach of all is to do formal practice based on compassion and the intention to liberate every being from samsara. Whenever we bring forth good heart, purehearted helpfulness, love, and compassion, such qualities, like a solvent, naturally purify and dissolve karma.

The great Indian Buddhist practitioner Asanga went into retreat in a cave and meditated night and day on Maitreya Buddha. After six years, he hadn't had a single auspicious dream or vision—no sign of accomplishment. So Asanga decided that his meditation was futile. He left his cave and as he walked down the road passed a man rubbing a silk scarf on an iron pillar. Asanga asked the man, "Sir, what are you doing?"

"I'm making a needle," the man replied.

Asanga thought, "Oh, such perseverance! He's rubbing an iron pillar with a silk scarf to make a needle, and I don't even have enough patience to stay in retreat." He walked back to his cave and started meditating again, night and day, on the Buddha Maitreya.

After three more years of meditation, he still had received no sign of accomplishment. No dream, no vision, nothing. Again, very discouraged, he left his retreat. As he walked down the road, he saw a man dipping a feather into a bucket of water and brushing it on the rock face of a huge cliff. Asanga asked the man what he was doing.

"This cliff is casting a shadow on my house," he replied, "so I am removing it."

Asanga thought, "Here is someone who, for just a little sunshine on his roof, would stand endlessly brushing a rock face away. And I can't even meditate until I get a sign." So he went back to his cave and sat down in meditation.

After a total of twelve years in retreat, he still had received no sign. Again, discouraged and disappointed, he left. Walking down the road this time, he encountered a very sick dog. The lower half of her body was rotten with gangrene and filled with maggots. Missing her two hind legs, she could only drag herself along the road. Yet she turned and snapped at everyone around her. Asanga's heart moved. "This poor dog," he thought, "what can I do to help her? I have to clean the wound, but then I might kill the maggots. I cannot take the life of one to preserve the life of another; every life has value."

Finally he decided that by carefully licking the maggots away from the wound he could save both the insects and the dog. It was a revolting idea, but he closed his eyes and leaned over. When he opened his mouth, his tongue touched not the animal but the ground. He opened his eyes. The dog was gone and there stood the Buddha Maitreya.

"I've been praying to you for years and years," Asanga exclaimed, "and this is the first time you've appeared!"

The Buddha replied very kindly, "From the very first day you began your meditation, I have been with you. But because of the delusion caused by your nonvirtue and the poisons of your mind, you couldn't see me. I was the man rubbing the pillar, I was the man brushing the cliff. Not until I appeared as this rotten dog did you have enough compassion and selflessness to purify the karma that prevented you from seeing me."

Karma can also be purified through our sincere confession and regret, utilizing the *four powers*. The first of these is the power of witness or support. We invoke the embodiment of perfection in whom we have faith, a particular aspect of enlightened being such as Tara, the embodiment of wisdom, or Vajrasattva, the deity of purification, as the witness for our practice.

The second power is that of sincere regret for all of our negative actions in this and every previous lifetime—regret not only for specific incidents that we remember, but for the whole backlog of harmful acts that we've committed since beginningless time.

The regret must be sincere, as if we suddenly realized we had mistakenly swallowed a deadly poison. We feel anguish over having acted for countless lifetimes in ways that will only result in suffering. We regret we have been careless, ignorant of the moral consequences of what we have done. We recognize these actions as harmful and accept responsibility for them.

The third power is the firm decision not to commit any negative actions in the future. We can't spend the day indulging in negative thoughts and actions and then, at night, expect to purify them with a little meditation practice. Instead, we must make a sincere commitment never to repeat them. A famous prayer in the Tibetan tradition states that without regret and a firm resolve, confession is not effective.

The fourth power is that of the antidote, the purification and blessing. We visualize nectar or rays of light flowing from the object of our faith through our body and purifying us, washing away all negativity, sickness, and obscurations.

In Buddhist India some centuries ago, a nun named Palmo was afflicted with leprosy. With no effective treatment known, her body began to rot and waste away. She repeatedly performed the two-day fasting ritual of the bodhisattva of compassion, Avalokiteshvara, a very strong purification practice. After a long period of time she had a vision of Avalokiteshvara and was completely cured. She had purified the karma that had resulted in her horrible disease.

In Tibetan medicine, there isn't an effective treatment for leprosy either. People with this affliction are isolated from everyone else and food brought to them is left at a distance. When a leper dies, nobody dares touch or bury the body. Instead, the dead leper's house is collapsed onto the corpse. A Tibetan lama with leprosy performed the same two-day fasting ritual of Avalokiteshvara a thousand times in succession and was cured.

Through diligent practice, aeons of karma can be purified in a single lifetime, whereas under normal circumstances the ripening and purification of karma are drawn out lifetime after lifetime.

Question: The killing of innocent children in war—is that their karma or is it something else?
Response: Generally, everything is the result of some kind of karmic predisposition or tendency. But that doesn't mean that all karmic tendencies are of equal force or equal urgency. Some are more powerful than others. Children who

are killed in war did nothing in their present lifetime to justify their death. But to have been born when and where they were, and killed under those circumstances, they must in a previous existence have created the karma to die in that way. This doesn't mean they deserved to die. But it explains why there are "innocent victims."

Question: There are so many beings and so much karma, how is it all arranged? How is it all kept track of? How does it all happen just right?

Response: It isn't a process that necessarily needs keeping track of. Actions work themselves out in their own way without anyone controlling the outcome. It is not as though someone has to keep a record of everything so that everyone goes to the right realm, and so forth. A being's actions determine that being's eventual experiences.

Question: Does karma always ripen in the same way?

Response: Karma is more complex than just one specific act always leading to one specific result. For example, there is what we call the *complete maturation* of a karmic tendency. Virtuous actions, those that contribute to the happiness of others, lead to the benefit of the person who performs them, either in this or in some future lifetime. Such actions contribute in general to rebirth in higher states of existence. Conversely, harmful acts that bring about pain and suffering, such as killing, mature as rebirth in lower realms.

There are also the karmic consequences known as *behavior in harmony with the initial action.* Take, for example, a being, such as a predatory animal, a hunter, or a soldier, who kills many living things. The complete maturation of this tendency to kill is rebirth in a hell realm. Once the karma has been exhausted, that being, owing to other virtuous karma, may attain a human rebirth and yet still have a habit of killing. By taking the lives of many beings, such people create a predisposition or compulsion to take life; it seems to be a part of their character.

Then there is *experience that accords directly with the initial action.* For example, an individual may kill many beings and as a result be reborn in a hell realm. Much later, upon finding a human rebirth, that individual's life will be short or even terminated violently.

A single act has a multitude of potential consequences. It's not that we commit one act, and then go on to another realm and pay the consequences, and then come back again to the human realm. It's actually much more complicated than that.

What's important to understand is that whether we committed a harmful action in a previous lifetime or in this lifetime, we unavoidably created negative karma. We can't escape that fact, even though perhaps there are aspects of it we are not aware of right now.

Question: Considering how much negative karma I've generated in this lifetime alone, simply out of ignorance, not understanding the effects of what I was doing, it helps to know there are meditation practices I can do and that compassion and loving kindness will also purify karma. But what about all the nonvirtue we create everyday without meaning to, for example by eating meat or wearing cotton clothing when we know insects have been killed to harvest that cotton?

Response: It's true that, in order for us to eat or drink, other beings are often harmed. Some vegetarians think that they have no responsibility for the killing of living beings. Yet in the planting and harvesting of grains, vegetables, and teas, many animals that live in the ground are killed when the earth is turned over and they are exposed or crushed, and many others drown when crops are watered. We in the Tibetan highlands used to feel great compassion for the people of the lowlands who consumed a lot of grains and vegetables because of the many insects that died so they could eat. When we ate yak meat, a staple of our diet, only one being had to die to feed many people for many meals.

In the refugee camps in India where we lived after fleeing the Chinese occupation of Tibet, we worked in tea factories and saw many insects die as each leaf was pulled during the harvest. It's difficult to live without harming others. But we can begin by trying not to harm. In eating, either meat or vegetables, at least we haven't engaged in three of the four parts of nonvirtuous action: identifying the victims, establishing the motivation to kill them, or either ordering or enacting the killing. Our only nonvirtue is our rejoicing in the fact of their death through our consumption of the food, through which we share the nonvirtue of the person who actually caused the death.

In addition to not intentionally causing harm, we can dedicate whatever merit we create to all those beings with whom we have either a positive or negative connection—in this case to those with whom we have a negative connection through eating, drinking, wearing cotton—so that both temporary and ultimate benefit will arise for them. Then our relationship with these beings may become their connection to the path of liberation. We can even sponsor practitioners in retreat to do special purification practices and dedicate the merit of that practice to the beings we've harmed.

Once somebody asked a great practitioner about his past life, saying, "You must have been a very high lama or practiced great virtue to have developed such realization in this life." The practitioner replied, "Not at all. In my last life I was a goat with no previous connection to the dharma. But a great yogi prayed strongly on my behalf before eating my body, and my practice in this life is a result of those prayers."

Purifying karma through spiritual practice doesn't require leaving our worldly lives behind. Rather, by integrating practice into our daily activities, resting in mind's true nature, we can purify all our accumulated karma in one lifetime.

11 The Fourth Foundational Thought: The Ocean of Suffering

The results of all our actions form the tapestry of our lives, every thread, every detail. Each of us continues to weave different physical and environmental realities, binding ourselves more deeply to the cycles of suffering. Our experience depends on our karma, which produces differing degrees of delusion. If the poisons of the mind are acute, we endure a very painful, hellish reality. If the poisons decrease, our reality becomes less harsh, more pleasant.

The Buddha spoke of suffering in the same way we would speak of illness to sick people, simply to help them understand that they weren't well, that there was something wrong. If there were no cure for suffering, there would be no point in discussing it. But the fact that there is a cure makes it of paramount importance to recognize suffering as fundamental so we can begin to find that cure.

There are three kinds of suffering. The first is *suffering atop suffering*. One bad thing happens after another, and there seems to be no fairness to it. Whenever you think that the situation you're in can't get any worse, it does. Wealth is lost, family, youth—there are countless ways in which we suffer. The second kind is the *suffering of change*. Nothing is reliable or consistent. No matter how much we hope for a firm foundation to stand on, whatever we rely on always erodes, creating great pain. The third is *pervasive suffering*. Just as when you squeeze a sesame seed, you'll find that it's pervaded with oil, it may seem that our lives are happy, but when we get squeezed, we suffer. As surely as we're born, we will become sick, age, and die.

Within samsara, there are countless beings whose suffering is far greater than ours. Ninety-five percent experience a brutal reality. The lives of only five percent— humans, demigods, and worldly gods—are relatively fortunate. Yet we humans often bemoan our existence, complaining bitterly about our terrible problems. We would never feel this way if we had an appreciation for the tremendous degree of suffering in other realms. The very worst human experience is still a thousand times more bearable than what the least-suffering beings in the lower realms must endure. Their suffering is so excruciating we can scarcely imagine it; the length of time it lasts is unfathomable. For some beings, even death provides no escape until hundreds of thousands of years, sometimes aeons, have passed.

Most beings in these realms have no time to help themselves. Their suffering remains so intense, they haven't a moment's leisure to meditate or to examine themselves or their lives from a different point of view. Other beings, in higher realms, are intoxicated with pleasure. A false contentment has allowed them to settle into a state of inactivity. When their long life inevitably ends, they experience terrible suffering, for they haven't used their ample leisure to create conditions for future happiness.

The idea that we can experience realms of suffering we call hell makes many people skeptical or angry. They don't believe in hell; they think the concept is just a scare tactic some religions use to control people. In a sense, it's true that there is no hell. If we put all the world's technology to use trying to reach the center of the earth, we'd never find hell. Yet many beings are suffering in the hell realms at this very moment.

Hell is the reflection of mind's delusion, of angry thoughts and intentions and the harmful words and actions they produce. If these aren't controlled, there will be no way not to experience hell. Practitioners have to be careful; some might think, "My meditation is so profound I don't have to worry about karma." But the repercussions of delusion are infallible, and it doesn't take a lot of delusion to find oneself born in hell.

Some people experience hell even while in human bodies. Many of them fill our hospitals. There are people who are tormented by the belief that someone is trying to kill them or tear their flesh. There are some who experience being eaten alive or being trapped in a fire. We could be sitting in the same room with them and see nothing of what they endure.

At the same time, we might be standing right beside a great meditator who is experiencing heaven, the pureland, without seeing it ourselves.

Heaven and hell, in fact, aren't really so far apart. This is a bit tricky to understand, since the experience of heaven is very different from that of hell. But it makes sense if we consider the example of a simple substance like water. To humans, water is crucial for sustaining life; to fish, it's the environment; to worldly gods, an ambrosia-like substance; to hungry ghosts, blood or pus; to hell beings, molten lava. It's not that the substance itself differs in each case, but rather that different beings' perceptions and experiences of it vary. Just as our vision changes when we put on glasses of a different strength, our experience of reality is totally conditioned by our perception, which is determined by the extent of our delusion.

On a cosmic scale, the experiences of the six classes of beings in the three realms of existence (the desire, form, and formless realms)—the whole of cyclic existence—are collective dramas unfolding as expressions of the group karma of those beings. When we see a movie projected on a screen we invest it with a certain amount of reality, and for that reason we are affected by it. We become upset, over-joyed, terrified, or angered by what we see. It doesn't mat-ter if we know the origins of film or understand how it works. When we watch a movie, it changes us by evoking particular emotional states. We might take a step back and say that, ultimately speaking, there is nothing there, it's just a movie. But for the most part we remain totally absorbed in what we are watching. If a group of people sit in front of the same movie screen, they will be affected in more or less the same way. A comedy will make them happy; a horror movie will scare them. As human beings who share a col-lective reality called the desire realm, we find the strongest impulses in our minds to be desire and attachment and we see things in very similar ways.

Although great meditators can glimpse other realms, we have no absolute proof that even our human phenomenal world exists beyond our individual and collective minds. Still, just as we take our dreams to be real while we're sleeping, we hold the human realm to be real. And the five other realms are as real to the beings in them as our experi-ence is to us. Hell seems as real to a hell being, the hungry ghost realm as real to a hungry ghost, as the human realm seems to us. Ultimately, suffering comes not from the phe-nomena of those realms, but from the fact that beings in-vest them with reality.

Thus, it is not contradictory to say that our experience is real or true and at the same time false. Nor is it con-tradictory to say the same about any other realm. If we in-sist that the human realm is real, then all the other realms are real because the beings in them experience them as real.

The most acute suffering in all the realms is that of the

eighteen hells, the reflection and karmic consequence of anger and hatred and their expression in thoughts, words, and actions. The beings there suffer from extreme heat and cold. In the hot hells, flames the length of one's forearm cover the entire surface. With each step one's foot burns. When it's raised, it heals; then with the next step, it burns again. The fire blazes with an inconceivable intensity. Flames generated from the burning of pure sandalwood are said to be seven times hotter than ordinary fire, and seven times hotter still is the fire that will consume the universe at the end of this age; but the fire of the hot hells is seven times hotter than even that.

The bodies of hell beings are not the same as ours. Our flesh-and-blood body has a certain level of tolerance; it can stand or feel only so much pain. But hell beings, whose bodies are as sensitive as the eyeball, do not faint, lose consciousness, or die until their karma is finished.

In one hell, images of whomever one has killed—whether a deer, an insect, or a person—arise as large as mountains and crush one between them. As they separate, one's body becomes whole once more, only to be crushed again, and so on indefinitely. In another hell, beings are born with a line down the length of their body along which they're cut in half by a saw. The two halves grow together, only to be cut through again, and so on.

In the cold hells, the frozen environment, desolate, brutal, offers neither clothing nor shelter. Whereas humans fall asleep and die when they freeze, beings in this bone-cold realm, no matter how frozen they become, don't die until their karma is exhausted. Their bodies crack like meat left too long in a freezer.

Hundreds of times more horrific than any other realm, hell is quite simply the worst place to be.

Hungry ghosts suffer from intense hunger, thirst, and exposure to the elements. Again, this realm is not simply a metaphor, but very real to the beings trapped there, for they are constantly starving and burning with thirst. Their very bodies are structured to create pain. They have enormous heads, as huge as mountains, and stomachs the size of valleys. Their necks are as small as a tiny horse hair, so nothing can get through their gullets. Their limbs are so emaciated they can't support themselves, and it's extremely difficult for them to get around to search for food. For the most part, hungry ghosts can only lie prone, and starve. If they do find some food, it is usually filthy or putrid, and if they manage to swallow it, it turns to fire in their bellies.

Extreme greed and attachment are the karmic causes for rebirth in the hungry ghost realm. As long as the karma sustaining their existence has not been exhausted, hungry ghosts are unable to die, despite their agony, which may continue for thousands of years.

In the animal realm, suffering results primarily from the predation of one species on another. Because animals constantly seek to kill and eat each other, they are perpetually afraid. Wild animals don't eat a single mouthful of grass without looking back and forth to make sure they're safe. The harsh treatment of animals domesticated by humans also causes great pain and suffering. Animals have very limited freedom; no matter how big and powerful the elephant, how pretty the peacock, they don't have the capacity to think something through and then act. This karma results from nonvirtuous actions motivated by ignorance and stupidity.

Virtuous actions stained by all the mind's poisons, with no one predominating, produce rebirth as a human being. Though, as we have seen, the conditions in this realm are relatively fortunate, nonetheless we know suffering from birth, old age, sickness, and death, from war, violence, famine, and, more subtly, unrequited desire.

Demigods have a pleasant environment, but they are plagued by jealousy and competitiveness and so are always engaged in strife, bloodshed, and warfare. Rebirth as a demigod is produced by virtuous actions stained by jealousy and competitiveness, by doing something helpful only to demonstrate that one has done more than, or is superior to, someone else.

In the worldly god realm, the karma of virtue stained by pride produces very wonderful conditions. Worldly gods never get dirty, never smell, never have to wash their clothes. The flowers that decorate their bodies keep forever fresh—until seven days before death. Then their flowers decay, their bodies get dirty and begin to smell, and they know they'll soon die. For seven days—the equivalent of three hundred and fifty human years—they endure the anguish of knowing which lower realm they're going to fall into. Finally, when the karma sustaining their existence is exhausted, god realm beings die.

Gods in the form and formless realms experience a crude kind of *samadhi,* or meditative absorption. Formless realm rebirth is produced by attachment to stability, form realm rebirth by attachment to clarity, and desire god realm rebirth by attachment to bliss. Though not terrible rebirths, they're still samsaric. Sooner or later, once the positive karma maintaining that existence has exhausted itself, their intoxication will end and they'll be reborn in some lower, more painful realm.

Once aware of the suffering and the limitations of cyclic existence, we become motivated to find a way out, just as when we realize we're sick, we seek medicine. Understanding that virtue and nonvirtue determine whether our experience is one of happiness or sorrow, pleasure or pain, we are left with a choice: we can either change our actions and develop virtuous qualities, seeking liberation for ourselves and all beings, or we can continue to create nonvirtue, perpetuating endless suffering.

When we really start to understand suffering, we begin to see samsara as a rotting swamp we've all fallen into. Our only desire becomes that of freeing ourselves and others. That attitude of seeking our own and others' liberation is a quality we term *renunciation,* a crucial element of our entry into the spiritual path.

Through continuous contemplation of our precious human existence, death and impermanence, karma, and suffering, the mind is turned toward the dharma. If you can see through the three poisons, the fuel of samsara, so that they no longer hold sway in your mind, then these four contemplations have done their job. If not, keep reflecting on the four thoughts until they're part of you, until they have fundamentally transformed your view of the world.

12 How to Contemplate the Four Thoughts

Each of us is like someone standing on the edge of a crumbling cliff, the earth rapidly breaking away. If we tell ourselves, "I'm too hot, too tired, too sick, too busy to do my practice," it's like saying we can't make the effort to move away from the ground that crumbles beneath our feet. It means we don't understand the four thoughts. Once we fully comprehend them, we'll realize the necessity of jumping clear. What's more, when we see someone else close to the edge and about to fall, we'll rush to help; we won't claim we're too tired or busy.

To arrive at this understanding, it's necessary to reflect on the four thoughts, to examine them critically, to ask ourselves, "Is it true that I have no alternative but the practice of dharma to break out of the unending cycles of existence?" Through repeated contemplation, or what is sometimes called *analytical meditation,* we can change our deeply ingrained thought patterns. If we didn't contemplate, the same old mental poisons—ignorance, attachment, aversion, jealousy, and pride—would come up day after day, year after year. Simply trying to quiet the mind isn't enough to overcome them. That kind of meditation practice is like pushing the "pause" button on a tape recorder so we won't have to listen to music we don't like. For as long as we hold the button, we don't hear anything, but as soon as we release it, the music we so dislike starts playing again. In contemplation, we do more than interrupt the tape—we erase it and make a new one. We transform our ordinary habits of mind, as well as negative thoughts and actions. Then we hear a different sound—one far more harmonious and beneficial.

The ordinary mind is like a legless man, while the winds, or subtle energies of the body, are like a blind wild horse. This combination of mind and winds is what can make meditation so difficult. In our practice, therefore, we address both aspects of the mind—its knowing quality and its quality of movement.

Taming the mind can be likened to taming a wild horse. Instead of tying a horse tightly to a short tether, which might frighten it and cause it to hurt itself trying to get free, we put it in a very large corral. It's not really free, but it doesn't feel confined because it has freedom of movement. As we spend more time with the horse, as it gets to know us and realizes that we're not going to harm it, it slowly loses some of its fear and we can come closer. As it begins to calm down, we can gradually make the corral smaller.

Similarly, when we want to tame the mind, we shouldn't try to restrain it at first, because it will react and jump around like a horse on a short tether. Instead of leaving thoughts wild and uncontrolled, we make a large corral of virtuous thoughts, transforming negative thoughts to positive ones. The mind isn't really free, yet it isn't completely confined. This way, we work with mind's qualities of movement, its unceasing display.

In addition to analytical meditation, we practice a more nonconceptual kind in which we simply let the mind relax and fall into its natural state, without any contemplation. Here we cut the mind's attachment to concepts, its habit of always thinking of past or future, likes and dislikes—as if constantly stirring the water in a muddy pond, never letting it settle and clarify. In so doing, we work with mind's self-seeing, or self-knowing, quality.

In this way, we utilize two principles of Buddhist practice. The nonconceptual technique is called *shamatha* in Sanskrit or *zhinay* in Tibetan. *Zhi* means "to pacify obscurations" and *nay* "to maintain"—referring to the calm, tranquil abiding where discursive and distracting thought patterns are pacified and the mind comes to rest one-pointedly.

The contemplative technique, using the rational mind in a skillful, inquiring way, is called *vipashyana* in Sanskrit or *lhagthong* in Tibetan, which means "deeper insight," seeing beyond ordinary seeing. Together these two are like the handle and blade of a sword with which we cut through to the quick our holding to the apparent solidity of subject–object experience. We sever the tight bonds of attachment, ego clinging, and self-importance, thus conquering afflictive emotions and ignorance.

In utilizing both methods, we work toward resolving duality by cutting attachment not only to the ordinary thought process, but also to nonconceptual, blissful, or extraordinary experience. In so doing, we cut the roots of the grosser reflection of the mind's poisons—samsara—as well as the subtler reflection of the mind's positive qualities—nirvana. When we alternate these two methods, slowly and subtly our perspective begins to change. What starts as intellectual understanding gradually becomes more personal and experiential. We approach the true nature of mind beyond the extremes of "is" and "isn't," thought and no-thought.

To attain enlightenment, we need both *shamatha* and *vipashyana;* neither by itself is sufficient. A bird needs both wings to fly—we need both method and wisdom, contemplation and relaxation. If we're tempted to believe that we can attain enlightenment or even happiness simply by thinking, no matter how methodically or intelligently, we need only remind ourselves that from beginningless time we've been thinking, so much so that our ideas could fill volumes. Yet they haven't made us any happier; they certainly haven't led us to enlightenment. If thinking alone produced enlightenment, we would already be buddhas.

Yet having a blank mind doesn't produce enlightenment either. Attachment to meditative stability can lead to a blissful existence for aeons in a formless realm in which there is no thought and no physical body, but once the karma sustaining that existence is exhausted, the mindstream falls into a lower realm, to suffer once again. Bears and prairie dogs hibernate for months at a time, yet their state of blank mind doesn't produce enlightenment.

The process of allowing the mind to rest is an effortless one that reveals an indwelling awareness, an awareness that is nondual, not a subjective awareness of an object. Usually, when people meditate, they try to *do* something. But instead of trying, simply let the mind relax, and rest in the free and spontaneously open space in which thoughts arise and subside. Thoughts of past, present, and future will naturally occur, but don't grasp at them, follow them, suppress or push them away. When thoughts arise, they almost invariably stem from ignorance, attachment, or aversion. Their recurrence in the mindstream forms the basis for the continuity of samsara, so instead of being upset when they come up, respond to them with compassion, realizing that this is how you and all other beings become entrapped in suffering. Thinking, "There's a thought—I have to get rid of it" is like the pot calling the kettle black, for both are thoughts. The goal is neither to think nor not to think. The goal is to reveal the essence of mind.

In the beginning, the mind won't stay relaxed for very long, because the habit of conceptualization is too strong. Instead of getting caught up in ordinary thoughts, contemplate the persistence of the thought process itself and use it to turn the mind back to dharma. Redirect your ordinary thinking in the following step-by-step process.

Begin by contemplating one of the four foundational thoughts, and then relax the mind. Then pray to the lama, or other object of your faith, for the blessing to accomplish something of benefit for yourself and others before impermanence intervenes and you no longer have this body. Generate compassion for the predicament of beings and offer the wish that all will attain liberation from the cycles of suffering. Then make a commitment to apply your understanding and the methods of dharma diligently in order to accomplish this. Then continue with contemplation of the next foundational thought, again rest the mind, then pray, generate compassion, and, finally, reiterate your commitment to free all beings from suffering, and so forth. In following this process, you will come closer to the direct experience of mind's nature, the absolute truth, which cannot be grasped by words or concepts.

Meditating in this way will prevent practice from becoming stagnant, like the film that forms on milk when it's left out in an open dish. We keep it fresh at each step. The key to meditation lies in cutting: after contemplating, we cut our attachment to concepts by relaxing. Then we cut our attachment to relaxation in order to pray. We pray, then we cut; we develop compassion and cut; we reestablish our commitment and cut to the next contemplation. This way, the mind won't fall into ordinary samsaric thinking, and we'll stay alert and concentrated in the quick of the experience. Meditation becomes fresher as it moves, like stream water as it tumbles, beating against one rock and then another, so that by the bottom of the cascade it's very pure.

Awareness of mind's true nature and the thought pro-

cess are not mutually exclusive. In fact, they are inseparable—a good practitioner never loses awareness while eating, driving to work, or playing with the children. The real
skill in meditation lies in not losing awareness in the moment of transition from one thought or activity to another.
By being fully present with each experience and each transition, you remain close to their essence. It's like riding a
wave. You stay right in the center of the movement, with
the force of the wave as it rises and falls. If you get ahead
of or behind it, if you get separated from it, you fall—you
lose it. In this way, you can learn how to ride the wave of
the thought process while not losing awareness.

The Sutra of the Bodhisattva Essence of Space contains a
dialogue between a bodhisattva, Namkhai Nyingpo, and the
Buddha Shakyamuni. The bodhisattva asks the Buddha,
"What is the spiritual meaning of freedom and opportunity?" The Buddha replies, "When the mind is distracted
by discursive thought, there is busyness and activity. When
the mind experiences peace due to the calming of discursive thought and the subsiding of that thought into the basic space of mind, there is leisure."

In addition to the "outer" sense of leisure—having the
opportunity to practice—there exists this "inner" sense of
leisure, the unique human possibility of experiencing the
natural relaxation of the mind, the falling away of discursive thought. Until we experience leisure in that inner
sense, our dharma practice won't be very effective, because
we will be perpetually distracted by thoughts and concepts.

Another method for deepening our understanding of the
four thoughts involves visualization. Begin by establishing
pure motivation, your aspiration to attain enlightenment in
order to help beings go beyond suffering and find per-

manent bliss and happiness. Then, in as much detail as you
can, consider how things change. When your mind becomes weary, relax. Don't force it; true relaxation doesn't
last very long at first.

When thoughts begin surfacing again, visualize yourself
in very high, rugged terrain where sheer black rock cliffs
rise precipitously. There's nothing to cling to. Only one
very narrow and precarious path snakes along the steep
sides of the cliff. The path grows narrower as you go, until
it completely disappears. You can't move forward, and behind you, chasing you, are snarling, ravenous beasts.
There's no safety anywhere, no place to hide. The beasts
close in from behind, and you've got nowhere to run.
You're helpless, without friends, without family, without
hope.

In desperation, you call upon your teacher, upon God or
Buddha—something greater than you, something infallible.
That embodiment of perfection appears, saying, "Have no
fear. These treacherous black cliffs have arisen as the result
of your clinging from beginningless time to a belief in the
truth of ordinary reality. This belief has become so strong
that your danger is great. Ignorance makes the landscape
dark. These beasts who mean to kill you represent ripening
karma you've created with your own poisonous mind. This
narrow path that disappears into nothingness is the way of
samsara. Whatever has come together will separate. Whatever is happening now will at some point cease. Day by
day, each step you take, left foot, right foot, will pass without any possibility of reclamation or control. The shortness
of the path indicates the brevity of your karma for remaining in this human life."

Then the infallible being you've invoked asks: "What is
death? What is samsara? It seems good, bad, happy, sad,

but it's like a dream. There's not a trace in it of anything true or solid. Delusion and ignorance perpetuate phantom experiences of danger and power. To awaken from this dream is to realize the birthless and deathless absolute nature."

After you've finished the visualization, let the mind rest. Finally, dedicate the merit of your practice to all beings, that they may awaken from the suffering dream.

Through this meditation, you will see that delusion, ignorance, poisons, karma, and the belief in the truth of an insubstantial reality all create the precarious conditions of the cycles of suffering. By recognizing impermanence and contemplating the empty, dreamlike nature of samsara, you will undermine your belief in the solidity of experience.

Meditation on the four thoughts brings maturity to our spiritual path. Without it, what we have is "fair weather practice." There's a Tibetan saying that as long as the food tastes delicious, the clothing is warm, the sun shines, and everything seems to be going fine, our practice will be reliable. But as soon as something goes wrong, a friend turns on us, we lose something or someone dear, it goes out the window. It doesn't support us in times of need or provide refuge from pain and fear.

Our practice needs to be stronger and swifter than the mind's obscurations. Otherwise, we'll only continue to indulge anger, desire, and ignorance, and they'll become more deeply ingrained. It's like riding downhill on a bicycle. In order to take control, we have to pedal faster than the pedals are already turning. In the same way, we have to work fast to avert the rapidly spinning negativities that are quickly taking us downhill.

Body, speech, and mind and the precious opportunity they offer are no more lasting or real than a bubble, no more permanent or substantial than a dream. We have to seize the moment, before it's lost and impermanence takes its toll.

Question: What's the difference between cutting and squelching? If you're meditating and you start to experience love or bliss, are you supposed to just squelch it?
Response: You don't have to try to get rid of bliss. But when the focus of your mind moves to compassion, the bliss naturally dissolves.

Bliss, clarity, and stability are naturally by-products of meditation, but they can become obstacles to meditation and to the path of enlightenment if we get attached to them. So the cutting process is crucial.
Question: When thoughts and emotions arise while we are meditating or dreaming, do they sow karmic seeds?
Response: For an action to have full karmic consequences, four elements must be present: the basis for action (the object); the motivation of the agent; the action itself; and its results. If one of these elements is missing, then the seriousness of the karmic consequences is diminished. But, even so, the action is not karmically neutral.

Although dreams are not as powerful as waking experiences in their capacity to generate karma, they nevertheless do so. As long as there is intent in the mind, some accumulation of karma results that must be confessed and purified, whether or not it actually translates into physical or verbal action. That is why we need to address the mind, for once we have eliminated negative intention, there will no longer be any basis for negative speech and action.
Question: So all of samsara is really full of suffering?
Response: If you look clearly at samsara, you'll find that there is no lasting happiness anywhere. There isn't anything

to base hope on. There aren't any samsaric circumstances you could mastermind through your virtue that would produce lasting happiness.

People often squirm when they hear this; it makes them very uncomfortable. But we need to think about it, because it causes us to realize that the spiritual path, difficult as it may be, is our only alternative.

If we travel the spiritual path very diligently, if our practice is pure and strong, we can purify karma. We need to contemplate the four foundational thoughts to inspire diligence, to ensure that we're not just making futile gestures or practicing a kind of pseudo-spiritualism.

We don't want to be like Tibetan moogoots, humanoid animals not unlike the American Sasquatch or Bigfoot. Moogoots are shy and keep to themselves in the forest. Hiding among the trees, they watch the farmers till the ground. When the farmers go home for the night, the moogoots come out and mimic their activities. They don't know what they are doing, so they beat the ground, stomp on things, and generally do a lot of damage. What they don't do is farm. We don't want to follow their example, mimicking the actions of spiritual practitioners, when all we're really doing is thrashing around and wrecking things.

By thinking about the preciousness of the human body and impermanence, we cut through our attachment to our worldly experience. When we understand that, no matter where we're born in samsara, great difficulties will arise and that all happiness is temporary, we cut through our complacent belief that it's enough to be born in a higher realm. We begin to develop the unwavering intention to achieve enlightenment instead of settling for ordinary rebirth, which will only perpetuate our confusion.

Think, relax, pray, generate compassion, renew your commitment. Pray to work ceaselessly to liberate all beings from the cycles of suffering. Pray to develop the ability to release all beings, wherever they are, into the truth of the absolute nature.

There was a very great practitioner in my family, Tulku Arig, one of my cherished teachers. People came from hundreds of miles just to look at the place where he meditated. Even the Chinese Communists said, "If you practice dharma the way he does, it's okay." He owned only what he could carry on his back and lived in a cave or small meditation house. His practice was very pure and simple. From the age of thirteen until his recent passing at the age of eighty-four, he slept only one hour a night because it was more important to him to practice than to sleep.

As a teacher he could be quite wrathful, directly confronting his students' attachments and aversions. When students came to him, for the first four years he taught them nothing but the four thoughts. He demanded that they penetrate the meaning and understand the consequences of these teachings until their mindstreams changed and their practice matured.

When people begged Tulku Arig to give more profound teachings, he said, "This teaching may not be good enough for you, but it was good enough for the buddhas. They meditated for years in order to understand the truth of the four thoughts. If this teaching is not profound enough for you, go somewhere else."

If you really understand the four thoughts, then you can meditate. But don't think that meditation is a piece of cake. When the great yogi Milarepa was asked, "How hard is your practice?" he replied that it was harder than carrying salt from the lake beds. To transport salt in Tibet, one filled a wet yak skin with wet salt and pressed it until the skin bulged, then let it dry. The drying yak skin would squeeze the packed salt, turning it into a hard rock. Milarepa said it was easier to carry such rocks of salt up and down a mountain all day long than to meditate.

If we intend to go beyond karma and the cycles of suffering, we have to meditate with tremendous intensity throughout our daily lives. We need to understand beyond doubt that there is no getting around karma, that there is no lasting happiness anywhere in samsara, that what we humans have right now is the greatest opportunity of all, and that it's short-lived.

It's as if we had fallen off a cliff, grasped a protruding branch, and were dangling in midair: we have no time to waste, no time for a coffee break. It's one thing to fall down and die once. But when we fall into hell, we keep dying. A one-time death is a human luxury. If we don't value this human opportunity, we won't use it before the branch gives way.

Don't deny the truth of the four thoughts. They may be hard to swallow, but don't fool yourself. Think about them. Contemplate them. Fathom what they mean and experience what they provide for meditation. They are called the supports to meditation, like the four posts of a platform you sit upon. They are transformative: they turn the mind toward the dharma, toward truth.

Part III

Refuge and Bodhicitta

13 Refuge

We know that our contemplation of the four thoughts has been effective if we begin to see through our samsaric experience, to understand that it lacks essence, that nothing within it is reliable or unchanging. What, then, can we count on? Where will we find true heart, true essence? Only in the sacred dharma, the spiritual path, will we discover something of absolute value.

The four thoughts fall into the category of introductory teachings called the *ordinary preliminaries,* common to all Buddhist traditions. Although foundational to the practice of dharma, they don't constitute a formal step in the Buddhist path. In order to go further, we need to make a commitment, embodied in the refuge vow. This is the first gate to Buddhist practice.

The word "refuge" connotes a place of safety or protection. In essence, the vow of refuge involves making a commitment to go the way of harmlessness. It's not that, once we take refuge, the Buddha or some other enlightened being waves a magic wand and suddenly we're beyond pain or dissatisfaction. Rather, we ensure our own protection by addressing the root of suffering, which lies in our own harmful thoughts and actions. If we reduce these through the disciplined use of body, speech, and mind, we avert their negative karmic consequences and thereby eliminate the causes of suffering.

The motivation for taking refuge in the Mahayana and

Vajrayana Buddhist traditions is selfless compassion for the limitless beings suffering in cyclic existence and a sincere desire to attain liberation in order to free them. The vow of refuge lasts not only for this lifetime, but until we attain enlightenment, however far in the future that may be.

We take refuge in the Three Jewels—the Buddha, dharma, and sangha. The Buddha is like one who has walked a certain road and, by virtue of having reached the destination, knows the route and can show us the way. The road itself is the dharma. And those with whom we travel, those who offer us support and on whom we rely, comprise the sangha. In taking refuge, we follow in the footsteps of those before us who have walked the path to enlightenment.

Taking refuge requires that we have an appreciation for the qualities of the Three Jewels, beginning with those of the infallible, enlightened Buddha. Many great saints and teachers have founded spiritual paths throughout the world, but they haven't possessed the attributes of the Buddha Shakyamuni. Having completely purified the afflictive emotions, karma, habit, and intellectual obscurations, the Buddha exhibited the thirty-two major and eighty minor marks of enlightened body, the sixty qualities of enlightened speech, and the two omniscient qualities of enlightened mind. His 112 marks of physical perfection—for example, a radiance apparent to all and the fact that his feet didn't touch the ground—were a direct and unmistakable display of perfect realization. Those who came in contact with the Buddha were awestruck by his presence; they knew they had encountered an extraordinary being. He didn't have to proclaim himself a teacher—it was obvious.

That sixty melodious tones marked the Buddha's speech doesn't mean he had a beautiful singing voice or was a good orator. Rather, his speech functioned as a perfect vehicle for communication. All of those who listened to a single teaching by the Buddha, no matter how vast the audience, heard perfectly, without amplification, a wealth of wisdom in their own language, as well as answers to their own particular questions.

The Buddha's mind was imbued with two kinds of knowledge: an omniscient, detailed, and discriminating awareness of phenomena on a conventional level, and a profound awareness of the true nature of reality.

In acknowledging these qualities, we recognize the Buddha as an infallible teacher who for countless aeons practiced harmlessness and helpfulness, purified karma, accumulated merit and wisdom, and thus gained the fruit of enlightenment. The Buddha, like a raw diamond, underwent the process of being cut, ground, and polished, becoming a brilliant, perfectly finished gem. The rest of us, though we have the same potential to become such gems, are still raw diamonds, rough, our perfect qualities obscured.

In taking refuge, we rely on the Buddha's example because, having accomplished the path, he has shown us the way. If we had to traverse a swampy marshland fraught with danger, someone who had already made the journey, who knew exactly what to avoid, who was sure of every step that must be taken, and who could lead us through flawlessly, would be a supremely valuable guide. The Buddha is such a guide. He has shown us what to abandon and what to embrace, pointing out the direction to take and demonstrating every step on the path to enlightenment.

Second, we take refuge in the sacred dharma: the teachings of the Buddha and the methods he used to achieve enlightenment—a great multiplicity of means, complete and without error, which are his legacy. Here, everything is clearly spelled out: the foundation, path, and fruit of practice, how to begin, how to overcome hindrances, how to enrich the positive qualities that begin to develop. These methods, or *yanas* (vehicles), are generally divided into nine categories, comprising three basic approaches: the Hinayana path of personal salvation, the Mahayana path of those seeking liberation for all beings, and the Vajrayana teachings within the Mahayana, often referred to as the *short path*.

Third, we take refuge in the sangha, the many practitioners who have practiced the Buddha's methods and maintained his legacy in an unbroken verbal lineage—perpetuating a historical record of the scriptures that enshrine the teachings—and in the mind-to-mind lineage—a vibrant tradition of personal experience that reveals the truth of these teachings. Because every generation since the Buddha has produced some individuals devoted to realizing the teachings, the dharma has not become dry and intellectual, but remains fresh and alive. The sangha is like a living *mala,* or strand of prayer beads, a "string" of practitioners threaded together by their practice through the centuries, exemplifying the teachings and maintaining a vital tradition that is accessible to us today and will continue to be so for generations to come.

The Three Jewels, then, are a dependable source of refuge from our suffering, ignorance, and confusion. This safety cannot be provided by anyone or anything still caught within conditioned existence—no matter how famous, beautiful, powerful, wealthy, or influential.

The word "refuge," like many other terms in dharma, has three aspects. So far we have been discussing its *outer* significance. It also has *inner* and *secret* meanings, which we will touch on here and discuss more fully later.

In the Vajrayana tradition, the inner sources of refuge are the Three Roots—the lama, yidam, and dakini. They

are said to be the source of blessings, spiritual accomplishment, and enlightened activity, respectively.

The lama or spiritual teacher is the root of blessings in
that he or she imparts the knowledge, methods, and wisdom
that enable us to achieve liberation. The yidam, or chosen
meditational deity, is the root of accomplishment in that, by
our practice, we are able to realize the nature of mind.
Through the method of the meditational deity, we are able
to realize the dakini, the female principle of wisdom, from
which arises the accomplishment of enlightened activity.

The secret object of refuge is none other than the true
nature of mind, the essence of every being—whether human, animal, hungry ghost, or god—faultless buddha nature. This nature has two facets: the first, *dharmakaya,* the
absolute nature of mind beyond ordinary concepts, can be
likened to the sun; the second, *rupakaya* or form kaya, can
be likened to the sun's brilliant radiance, which occurs
naturally and without effort. This radiance, manifesting for
the benefit of others, has two aspects: the *sambhogakaya*—
the pure form manifestation perceptible to great practitioners—and the *nirmanakaya* manifestation that arises for
the benefit of those unable to perceive the sambhogakaya
expression.

In Vajrayana Buddhism, by relying on outer, inner, and
secret objects of refuge, we purify karma on an outer, inner, and secret level simultaneously. It's as if instead of cutting with one blade, we cut with three.

Our experience in the endless continuum of samsaric
suffering can be likened to that of a fly caught in a capped
milk bottle. In trying to escape, it may fly up and down, all
around, but it can't find a way out. Taking refuge with the
goal of attaining enlightenment to benefit all beings is like
removing the cap from the bottle. The fly may not find the

opening immediately, but eventually it will, and become free. Once we make the refuge commitment, we can be sure that samsaric suffering will no longer be endless for us.

But though we've taken refuge, we can't just sit back and wait for the Three Jewels to bless us. If we don't do any work to ripen ourselves, we won't be receptive to their blessings. Taking refuge involves making a personal commitment. It's not a casual thing, to be treated lightly, not something we change our minds about somewhere down the line. We are by and large indecisive creatures. We keep waffling, thinking that maybe this will work or maybe that, maybe we'll live here or perhaps there, never establishing a commitment and never really getting anywhere.

Suppose we wanted to reach a mountaintop and could follow a number of paths to get there. If we took a few steps up one path, then thought maybe the next would be better and went a few steps on that path, then decided the third would get us there faster, continuing indefinitely in that fashion, we would never get to the top. We would only circle around. When we take refuge, we make a personal decision about which path is right for us and a commitment to follow that path.

The thought of making this commitment sometimes makes people apprehensive. Yet such apprehension is like fear of taking an antidote after having swallowed poison. The time for doubting is before you swallow, not after. Taking refuge simply means accepting the fact that you have swallowed poison and making a decision to take the necessary medicine. It means saying to yourself, "This is it for me. I am committed to not harming others. That is definite. I am committed not simply to working for my own benefit, but to benefiting others. I am certain about that. Until now I haven't paid much attention to my mind. I haven't really examined its nature or the way it works. But from now on I will be mindful and alert; I'll keep a firm watch. I will make an effort to accentuate and encourage that which is virtuous in me and to reverse and eventually eliminate my nonvirtuous tendencies." Only that kind of immovable commitment makes the vow of refuge effective.

The benefits of taking refuge in this way are truly incalculable. One of the scriptures states that if these benefits had tangible form, they would be larger than the entire three-thousand-fold universe. The term "three-thousand-fold universe" is not an insignificant one, for it represents a billion world systems ($1,000 \times 1,000 \times 1,000$). Through the blessings of our sources of refuge, we receive the guidance, the means, and the support for our spiritual practice and, ultimately, for achieving liberation. When our efforts meet these blessings, we can awaken to our intrinsic awareness, the true nature of our minds. And this is, in the deepest sense, what it means to take refuge.

Question: Once you're enlightened, can you ever go back? Are there stages to enlightenment or enlightenment experiences?

Response: There is really no such thing as an enlightenment experience. I've heard many people refer to this idea, but they don't really understand the meaning of liberation. To attain enlightenment, we need to purify the four obscurations—the poisons of the mind, intellectual obscuration, karma, and habit—and establish fortunate conditions through the accumulation of merit. Those who have done so manifest unmistakable qualities and create two kinds of benefit. The first, benefit for oneself—the removal of all obscurations and the recognition of one's intrinsic nature— is the realization of dharmakaya. The realization of our buddha nature liberates us from ignorance; and freedom from ignorance liberates us from the consequences of ignorance. The second, benefit for others, is the realization of the two form kayas, which are like the warmth and light given off naturally by the sunlike dharmakaya.

Once a woman addressing a panel I was on said that, three years before, she had been in a car accident. She felt she had become enlightened at that time and asked if we thought this was possible. Each panelist deferred to the next, until finally I questioned her, "Do you have anger?"

"Yes," she replied.

"Do you have desire?"

Again she said, "Yes."

"Then," I told her, "you don't have enlightenment."

In the course of meditation practice, one can have experiences of bliss, clarity, and/or stability, and it might be possible to construe these as enlightenment. But they're not. The qualities of enlightenment are truly different and unmistakable. One is no longer bound by samsaric mind or samsaric existence, and there is no possibility of losing that realization.

Question: What's the difference between making a commitment by formally taking refuge and simply not harming? Why is the formal commitment important?

Response: Suppose you make a commitment not to kill a dragon. Most people will never see a dragon in their entire lives; some think dragons don't exist. So, you might ask, why would anyone make a commitment not to kill a dragon?

If you never kill a dragon, you aren't creating any non-virtue, yet at the same time you're not creating any virtue. From the day you make a commitment not to kill a dragon, and continue to uphold that commitment, you're accumulating virtue. In taking refuge, you accumulate great virtue minute by minute as you uphold your vows.

14 Giving Rise to Bodhicitta

In order to direct ourselves along the spiritual path, we need a goal to work toward, as an arrow needs a target. Through bodhicitta, the next gate to practice in the Mahayana and Vajrayana traditions, we continue to aim at the target of enlightenment for the benefit of others every moment we practice. This is the best of all possible goals.

Bodhicitta is foundational to all we do, like the root of a medicinal tree whose branches, leaves, and flowers all produce life-enhancing medicine. The quality and purity of our practice depend on its permeating every method we use. With it, everything is assured. Without it, nothing will work.

This is why from the very first time we listen to the teachings we are told to establish the liberation of all beings as the purpose of our practice. We render ourselves fit vessels for spiritual teachings and practice by changing our motivation from one of self-interest to one of altruism.

Bodhicitta has three components: generating compassion for the suffering of all beings; aspiring to attain enlightenment in order to achieve the capacity to benefit all beings, called *wishing bodhicitta;* and actively engaging in the path of liberation in order to accomplish that goal, called *engaging bodhicitta.*

The Tibetan term for the Sanskrit *bodhicitta* is *jang chub sem. Jang* means the removal of obscurations, *chub* the revealing of all perfect qualities within, and *sem* mind. Through the

practice of bodhicitta mind, we purify obscurations and enhance our intrinsic positive qualities, revealing enlightened
mind.

Mind's obscurations can be compared to the clay cov-
ering a crystal that has long been in the ground. If we pick
up the encrusted crystal, it looks like a clay ball. Yet its
essential qualities are in no way reduced; they are only
obscured. If we wash away the clay, the crystal comes clear,
its qualities apparent. In the same way, by purifying and
removing the mind's obscurations, we reveal our true, crystalline nature.

We always look outside for this essence, though it lies
within. It's like searching everywhere for a lost horse, following countless hoofprints through the forest, only to discover, finally, that the horse has been in our basement all
along.

Compassion, the first aspect of bodhicitta, is also inherent within us. Although we naturally have good heart, it
is usually rather limited. Through practice, we can expose
and activate our own perfect, limitless compassion.

Jang chub sem is thus both a method and the fruit of
practice. Due to the momentum of bodhicitta, the force and
power of this intention to liberate beings, the sunlike essence of mind becomes completely revealed and benefit to
others arises spontaneously and effortlessly, like the sun's
reflection in every vessel and body of water.

We begin the practice of *jang*, the removal of mind's obscurations, by reducing our self-importance and redirecting
our attention to others. Our habit of focusing on ourselves
has been reinforced for countless lifetimes, which is why
we're trapped in samsara. Buddhas have eliminated selfish
and ordinary thoughts, developed selfless motivation, and
thus achieved enlightenment.

The development of this kind of motivation rests on

four cornerstones called the *four immeasurable qualities*. The first is equanimity, an attitude of equality toward all beings. If we can live free of prejudice or bias, without making a division in our minds between friends and enemies, then we have grasped the essence of existence and planted the seeds of our own and others' happiness and freedom.

Now our love and compassion extend only to certain people in certain kinds of situations, to our family, friends, and loved ones, but not to someone we perceive as an enemy. We may not wish unpleasant or dangerous people ill fortune, yet might have trouble not rejoicing if something bad happens to them. Our compassion for a sick child may derive simply from attachment to her. Through the practice of equanimity, we develop a noble attitude of compassion for all beings without distinction, from the depths of our heart. Unless we have this kind of purity of heart, our practice will remain superficial—we won't truly understand the purpose of dharma.

We develop equanimity, first, by realizing that all beings, equally, want happiness. Nobody wants to suffer. Second, we contemplate the fact that all beings, at one time or another through countless lifetimes, have been our own mother. The Buddha Shakyamuni and other buddhas and bodhisattvas, who removed the clay from the crystalline nature of their minds and became omniscient, taught that there is not a single being who has not been our parent, something we, too, could perceive if we so purified our mindstreams. Each being—no matter how antagonistic to us now—has been as kind and crucial to us as our parents in this lifetime. A person who now plays a seemingly insignificant or even a threatening role in our personal drama was once loving and helpful.

To develop an appreciation for this kindness, we need to recognize the enormous generosity of our parents. First and foremost, they gave us the gift of a human body. When, upon death in our last incarnation, our mind was plunged into the bardo, the frightening and chaotic intermediate state between death and rebirth, we were blown about helplessly, like a feather in the wind, without any stable frame of reference or support, experiencing terrifying sights and sounds. We finally found safety in our mother's womb at the moment of conception. From then on, our mother carried us in her body for nine or ten months, putting up with discomfort and perhaps illness to give us our human birth.

When we were helpless in our cradle, our mother provided care and protection so that we could grow strong and healthy. Had she not nurtured us, or asked another to do so, we would surely have died.

She saved our young life again and again, protecting us from falling, from eating things that would make us sick, from coming too close to fire, water, traffic. She fed and clothed us, washed us, and kept our home clean. Think how much we would have to spend now for someone to clean our house or to cook for us. These days, when someone gives us a cup of tea or some trifle and doesn't ask for payment, we think that person is tremendously kind. But such kindness pales in comparison with the generosity of our mothers.

Our ability to speak, to conduct ourselves in society, to get along with people are all gifts from our parents. Rather than be satisfied with our own cleverness, we should remember that there was a time when we didn't know how to say a single word, didn't know how to wipe, feed, clothe, or clean ourselves. Word by word our mothers and fathers taught us to speak. They helped us learn to walk, to eat, to dress. They were our first teachers.

In this and countless previous lifetimes, beings have shown us kindness in all these worldly ways. They have also been essential to our spiritual development in that their liberation is the purpose of our practice, the foundation of our altruistic motivation, without which we could not attain enlightenment. Considering such things, we begin to experience a profound sense of gratitude and an awareness of the debt we owe.

So in cultivating equanimity, we acknowledge that all beings have been our mother at some time. Then we develop an appreciation for the kindness they have shown us and a wish to repay them. In this way we develop a higher motivation, that of benefiting all beings, not only on a temporary basis, but with the most perfect form of repayment possible: attaining enlightenment so that we might help others to do the same.

A Western student once asked a lama, "I have a problem with thinking of beings as once having been my mother. My mother was never good to me. We had a bad relationship. So every time I sit down to meditate on bodhicitta, I think of my mother and get upset and angry. Can I just forget thinking about my mother for now?"

The lama told this man that the idea was to develop compassion for everybody, including one's mother, but that it didn't matter what order one did it in. He said that in Tibet and India people regard the mother as the kindest, most wonderful person imaginable. When a beginner needs an easy entrance into practice, the teacher uses those feelings for the mother as a basis for developing warmth and compassion for others.

The lama added, "If you find that a better approach for you is to develop compassion for all other beings first, and then for your mother, that's all right. The point is ultimately to have compassion for everybody, including your mother."

Finally, we recognize the equality of all beings in that

the intrinsic nature of each one, from the smallest insect to the greatest realization holder, is primordial purity.

Having come to understand this equality—in that all want to be happy, all suffer, all have shown us the kindness of parents, and all have buddha nature—we generate compassion for every one of them by recognizing their tragedy: that although they want only to be happy, out of ignorance they create conditions that perpetuate their suffering.

Compassion itself, the aspiration that suffering cease, is the second immeasurable quality. A powerful antidote to self-importance and self-interest, compassion helps us in the short term by releasing our relentless focusing on ourselves and our problems. And it is beneficial in the long run because even one or two minutes of heart-felt compassion purify enormous amounts of karma.

How do we generate compassion? We begin by contemplating the difficulties of others, and then we put ourselves in their shoes. We start with the suffering in the human realm, because it might at first be difficult to contemplate the anguish of beings in other realms.

We contemplate the distress of one or two people we know, and slowly, with practice, expand our focus to include more and more, until the suffering of everyone has true meaning for us. We recall the pain of these people so vividly that we can practically see it before our eyes.

Imagine, for example, someone close to you dying, perhaps in a hospital, surrounded by family and friends. When their suffering becomes very real to you, put yourself in their place. Your cherished family and friends are crying, pleading with you not to die. The doctor has told you that you have only a few minutes to live. Breathing is becoming difficult and you're terrified. You don't know what awaits you. Everything familiar, even your own body, will be left behind. Not a penny of the money you've accumulated will go with you, not a single friend or family member will follow, no matter how dear they might be to you and you to them.

Or instead of contemplating the misery of a person you know, you might imagine someone living in a drought-ridden country where families, even entire villages, are dying of starvation. Put yourself in that person's place. Picture yourself among the few beloved family members who haven't already died, who are lingering on the brink of death. You know that you, too, will soon die; there is simply nothing left to eat. You feel too weak to help your surviving relatives, and they are too weak to help you. You are all powerless in the face of death.

You might imagine someone dying in war and then put yourself in that person's place. Your best friend has been killed, is lying next to you, and you yourself are wounded, bleeding to death, and can't move. Everyone around you is dying or too busy to notice you. You feel completely alone and terrified.

Or you might contemplate the plight of an elderly person. Envision a time when your own children, whom you've carefully raised for so many years, won't help or even listen to you. Perhaps they're looking forward to your death. You can no longer care for yourself, nor do your children care for you. Perhaps you're alone in a nursing home where your children visit only once or twice a year. Your friends don't respect you any longer; they won't listen to you anymore. You would like to move, act, talk as you did when you were younger, but you lack the capacity to do so.

As you examine each of these situations, tremendous fear will arise. At that point, ask yourself, "If I feel this much fear simply from contemplating such suffering, how must those who actually experience it feel?"

Then think about the fact that many people throughout

the world are hurting others. They're creating negative karma that will eventually bring them harm, and they don't even realize it. They think they're doing the right thing, but they're only destroying themselves.

As you contemplate in this way, compassion and the aspiration to help both those currently suffering and those planting seeds of future suffering will arise strongly in your heart. Acknowledge your own relative good fortune and then make the commitment to do everything you can to benefit. You have heard the teachings of the dharma; you have some methods for purifying the causes and conditions of suffering. But these beings, all of whom have shown you the kindness of a mother, have nothing. How tragic.

In Mahayana Buddhism, great compassion, equal compassion, for all beings—friends and enemies—is crucial. With this strong foundation, even if you don't try to attain enlightenment, it will lie in the palm of your hand. If, however, you don't develop compassion but are motivated only by the selfish desire to escape suffering yourself, you will not achieve the ultimate goal.

Compassion is enhanced by the third immeasurable quality: a love that reaches equally to all. Love is the sincere desire that each being experience both the cause and fruit of temporary and ultimate happiness. We establish a commitment to make every effort, physical, verbal, and mental, to bring this about.

When we strive toward the happiness of others, we must do so pure-heartedly. If there is some self-purpose in our efforts, failure will cause us regret, and this regret will nullify the virtue of our actions.

To help us develop the capacity for a pure and selfless love for all beings there is a method called *tonglen meditation*. We begin by generating compassion as we contemplate the painful condition of others. Then, as we inhale, we imagine we are breathing in the suffering and negative karma of all the realms of experience in the form of black light. As we exhale, we visualize all of our love, happiness, and good fortune radiating out to others as white light.

At first, you might feel reluctant to practice this meditation, fearing that it will harm you in some way. But if you have the selfless intention to help others, your doubts will vanish and the practice will increase your positive qualities. Only your fear itself can harm you, for it acts as a magnet for negativity.

After practicing this meditation strongly with pure heart, you will begin to see yourself as a vehicle for others' happiness. Not only will your love and compassion increase, but you will find yourself thinking fewer negative thoughts and committing fewer harmful actions; your self-clinging will begin to loosen, and your karma will be purified. Ideally, we develop the loving capacity of bodhicitta mind to such an extent that we would fearlessly, without hesitation or regret, give or do anything necessary to help another.

In many of his lifetimes on the bodhisattva path, the Buddha Shakyamuni gave up his body for the sake of others. In one lifetime, he was the middle of three sons of a king. While lost in the forest with his two brothers, he came upon a starving tigress and her five cubs. The tigress could no longer move and had no milk to feed her litter. The prince thought, "How many times in my past lives have I tried to save myself? I've thought only of my own safety, and died again and again without benefiting anyone. My body is impermanent; it won't last long anyway. If it can be of use to this tigress and her cubs, so be it."

He sent his brothers off to search for fruit and lay down next to the tigress. She was too weak, however, to feed on him. Having no knife, the prince broke a shoot of bamboo, slit his wrist with it, and let the blood drip into her mouth.

Then he cut off pieces of his flesh and fed them to her. As the tigress slowly gained strength, he lost more and more of his own. But he had no regret; he dedicated his life not only to the mother and her cubs, but to all other beings, and then he died.

At that moment, the boy's mother had a dream of three suns in the sky, the middle sun eclipsed. She awoke knowing that something had happened to her middle son, and witnessed extraordinary phenomena—the earth shook, flowers rained down, and music and songs of praise resounded.

The prince's hair and bones were placed in a *stupa*, a monument to the nature of mind, at a sacred site known as Namo Buddha in Nepal. Many people still derive great benefit, purifying vast amounts of karma, by circumambulating that *stupa*.

The last of the four immeasurable qualities is rejoicing: delighting in the happiness of others. We rejoice in others' worldly blessings—their health, wealth, wonderful relationships—and in their spiritual good fortune. We don't allow jealousy to overtake us, nor wonder, "Why do they get this or that, and not me?" Instead, we make the wish that their happiness will be long-lived, and we do everything we can to make that happen.

By rejoicing in others' virtue, we create as much as they have. In the same way, if we relish someone's misfortune, we create as much nonvirtue as the perpetrator of their misfortune.

During the time of the Buddha Shakyamuni, two boys were begging for food outside a king's palace. The king had invited the Buddha and his retinue to lunch, and a very wonderful meal had been prepared. One boy began to beg for food before the Buddha was offered any. Nobody gave him anything to eat and he became very angry. He thought,

"If I were a king, I'd chop off the head of the Buddha, and of this king, and of everyone who is helping him."

The other boy waited until the Buddha and his retinue had been served. Then he begged for leftovers and was given as much as he could eat. He thought to himself, "What a wonderful king. What great merit he has created by inviting the Buddha to lunch and by his generosity to those of us who are poor. If I were a king, whatever I had I would offer to the Buddha, as well as to the poor."

After lunch, the boys separated. The good-hearted boy wandered across the border into a nearby kingdom. He lay down to sleep, sheltered from the heat by the shade of a tree. Unbeknownst to him, the king of this region had died and his ministers were searching for someone with the qualities and merit to be the new king. The people in the village where the boy slept noticed that throughout the day, although the sun changed position in the sky, the shade never shifted from where the boy slept. Thinking this extraordinary, they reported it to the ministers.

When the ministers received this news, they ordered that the good-hearted boy be included among the candidates for the throne who were to appear at a large gathering of all the king's subjects. The new king would be chosen by a very special elephant. On the appointed day, the elephant approached the poor, bedraggled boy—who stood at the very back of the group of candidates—anointed his head with special water from a vase, lifted him up with his trunk, and placed him on the throne.

Meanwhile, the angry boy slept in the king's garden. A nearby chariot lost control and careened over his body, cutting his neck and killing him.

At first, practicing the four immeasurable qualities requires effort. One by one, we release the knots that bind us—the mind's poisons and delusions. Equanimity reduces pride, rejoicing reduces jealousy, compassion reduces desire, and love reduces anger and aversion. As anger wanes, mirror-like wisdom dawns; as desire wanes, discriminating wisdom dawns; and so forth. As our practice matures and wisdom is revealed, the four immeasurable qualities arise naturally, effortlessly, just as rays of light and warmth radiate from the sun.

Although many think they can recognize wisdom directly, it's not so easy. Until the knots begin to release, awareness will not be evident. It is through the four doors of love, compassion, joy, and equanimity that we can enter the mandala of the absolute nature of mind.

15 *Wishing and Engaging Bodhicitta*

Bodhicitta has two frameworks: that of the welfare of others, or compassion; and that of enlightenment, or wisdom. We wish for enlightenment not just to escape samsara but also to benefit whoever sees, hears, touches, or remembers us. Now we might have the capacity to help ten, a hundred, a thousand, or, if we're famous, perhaps a hundred thousand or even millions of people. But that isn't enough. A limitless number of beings suffer throughout samsara.

When we practice, we can give rise to one of three forms of bodhicitta. We call the first the *shepherd-like attitude,* in that our motivation is to lead all sentient beings to enlightenment ahead of us and to follow after them just as a shepherd herds his sheep through the gate, then follows after. We call the second the *ferryman's* or *boatman's attitude.* In crossing a river, the boatman arrives at the opposite shore at the same time as his passengers. In the same way, you and all other beings go together to enlightenment. Realistically, however, in order to free others from the cycles of existence, you must first free yourself. Just as a king assumes the throne first and then rules the kingdom wisely, in your practice you aspire to attain buddhahood yourself, so that you will be able to free others from samsara. This is known as the *kingly attitude.* We cultivate one or the other of these forms of bodhicitta to counteract various degrees of self-clinging, the greatest single impediment to enlightenment.

Aspiring to attain enlightenment for ourselves and all beings is called *wishing bodhicitta.* Although essential to our practice, it alone will not accomplish our goal. Wishing bodhicitta is like looking at the vast ocean of samsara and wanting to get ourselves and others to the opposite shore. If we don't have a boat and a means to propel that boat, no matter how much wishing we do, we won't get across.

We must also become actively involved—we have to actually enter the path of practice. Fully utilizing the methods that reduce and purify negative thoughts and actions, and that enhance positive qualities, and simultaneously recognizing the true nature of mind so that we can bring ourselves and all beings to buddhahood, is called *engaging bodhicitta.* This is the way of the bodhisattva.

One method of incorporating bodhicitta into every aspect of our lives is to practice the *six perfections,* or (in Sanskrit) *paramitas:* generosity, moral discipline, patience, diligence, concentration, and wisdom.

Generosity loosens our grip on the things we cling to. There is the material generosity of sharing food and clothing and other things of substance; the spiritual generosity of imparting spiritual teachings, of providing freedom from fear and protection for those who are afraid; and the generosity of effort, giving freely of our time and energy as well as our speech in sharing, teaching, counseling, and expressing loving kindness to benefit others. Whatever fortune we presently enjoy is the fruit of our past generosity, which we can now rejoice in sharing.

In the practice of moral discipline, we continually check our motivation to ensure that we use our body, speech, and mind skillfully, that we are not only truly harmless but helpful. In addition, we strive to create conditions that will enable us to produce the greatest benefit—learning what we need to learn, pulling together the necessary resources, and so on. Finally, we remain tireless in our discipline.

We practice patience by relentlessly pursuing our efforts to benefit others no matter what their reaction or their attitude toward us. We also develop patience as an antidote to aggression, anger, and hatred. A Buddhist proverb says, "For an evil such as anger, there is no practice like patience." It contributes to our peace of mind and ultimately to the attainment of enlightenment.

There are three basic kinds of patience: forbearance in the face of threats or harm from others, in accepting and dealing with the hardships of spiritual practice, and in accepting and relating without fear to the profound implication of the true nature of reality.

Patience can be applied on a personal, local, or national level. Whenever an individual or a group creates problems for others, instead of reacting to their aggression with anger, we should remind ourselves that all beings have been our mothers and shown us great kindness, that out of ignorance they neither understand this connection nor realize that they are planting seeds of suffering. By not responding in kind we benefit all those involved, because our forbearance very quickly diffuses aggression and we don't create further problems.

As the Buddha Shakyamuni sat under the bodhi tree in Bodh Gaya, India, the forces of Mara, the embodiment of all that binds us to samsara, in a last attempt to defeat him and prevent him from attaining enlightenment, called together a great host of demons. This demonic army attacked the Buddha, but by the power of his patience, love, and compassion, arising naturally from his realization, their weapons turned to flowers.

Diligence involves preparing for and beginning a task,

donning armor-like perseverance to see that task through, and, finally, never turning back. We develop not only inner qualities, but the means to benefit others. For example, someone may have abundant loving kindness and the intention to help sick people, but helping the sick first requires years of dedicated study and practice in the health professions.

We practice diligence in order to achieve our goal: the temporary and ultimate happiness of all beings. If it's not possible to move one step forward, at least we shouldn't back up. Slowly, step by step, even a donkey can make its way around the world.

We develop concentration, or meditative stability, by training the mind. The Tibetan term for this perfection is *samten, sam* meaning "to think," to use the rational mind in contemplation, and *ten* meaning "stable" or "firm." The experience of meditative stability is often equated with the Tibetan *zhinay,* where the mind comes to rest one-pointedly, either upon an idea or in the natural state of awareness.

One kind of meditative stability involves thinking about or focusing on a single idea without distraction so that the mind doesn't wander to other—even parallel—ideas. Concepts and the words that convey them point us to a deeper meaning. The mind falling naturally into its fundamental state, unobscured by thoughts of the three times—by memories, by thoughts of the present, or by anticipation of what may arise in the future—is another form of meditative stability. Yet another, more profound kind is imbued with the sixth perfection of wisdom, which acts as a seal applied to the calm state of abiding.

Wisdom, also called transcendent knowledge, means knowledge of absolute truth beyond ordinary concepts, object–subject duality, and temporary experiences of bliss, clarity, and stability. Beyond this, there is nothing to be known. Beyond this there is no goal.

The first five of the six perfections are subject–object oriented. In the case of generosity, for instance, we speak of the subject, oneself, who gives; the object, the person to whom something is given; and the act of giving. The subject, object, and the action between them are called the *three spheres.*

Belief in the solidity of the three spheres is the domain of relative truth. Reality has two aspects: ultimate reality, or absolute truth—things as they are in and of themselves— and relative reality, or relative truth—things as they appear to be on a conventional level. The Tibetan term for relative truth consists of *kun,* meaning "all" or "many," and *dzob,* "that which is not true." So *kundzob* implies the display of myriad phenomena that appear to be something they are not.

Like children chasing after a rainbow, we treat the dreamlike display of appearances as substantial and graspable. Yet nothing in those appearances is permanent. Nothing is singular—a hill, for example, consists of many things, like dirt, rocks, atoms, and molecules. And nothing is free— everything can be affected by something else.

We call these phenomenal appearances "truth" because, in the context of our dreamlike experience, so they seem. For instance, fire, while not permanent, singular, or free, will burn our flesh if we put our hand in the flames. In this sense, our relative experience is true. At the same time, the ultimate nature of experience remains unchanging and absolutely pure—empty, just as the night dream experience is empty. In the night dream, things appear to happen, yet when we awaken we see that nothing really occurred. This is the true nature of all samsara.

The great Shantideva of Buddhist India stated that ultimate truth is not the province of ordinary mind. Ordinary mind concerns itself with conventional reality, whereas ultimate reality remains free of and beyond all conceptual elaborations—one cannot say that things exist, nor that they do not exist, that they are or are not. As we hear teachings, contemplate, and meditate, our intellectual understanding gradually becomes a deeper knowing, a direct experience, and finally the stable realization of our ultimate nature. Then we discover, as a famous Tibetan prayer states, that the absolute truth is not some *thing* that exists, for even the Buddha cannot see it. Yet we cannot deny relative reality by saying that nothing exists at all, because how would we account for all samsara and nirvana—the unceasing display of phenomenal appearances? There is no contradiction in stating that the fundamental nature of things is changeless, though on the relative level it manifests as a changing, ephemeral display; that just as in a dream, phenomena do not ultimately exist, although they manifest. Because of this, we say that phenomena are *empty*.

The empty nature of our experience, the birthless, deathless nature in which nothing has ever come or gone, the nature beyond the extremes of existence and nonexistence, is inseparable from the unceasing display of manifest appearances. The actual nature of our relative experience is the absolute truth. We call the knowledge of the inseparability of absolute and relative truth *view*.

When we apply view to our practice of the first five perfections, we go beyond their ordinary meaning. If in a dream at night we give an apple to a beggar, in truth, there is no apple, no beggar. When our generosity is imbued with wisdom, the knowledge of the true nature of the three spheres, it becomes the perfection of generosity. Knowing, as we act to benefit another, that that action is empty of inherent existence, yet acting nonetheless, is the essence of the practice of the six perfections and of the path of the bodhisattva.

The act of benefiting is called the *accumulation of merit,* the effortful gathering of virtue. We harness the mind's duality using skillful methods such as the first five of the six perfections in a conceptual framework to create benefit within the relative dream experience. The effortless practice of awareness within a nonconceptual framework we call the *accumulation of wisdom.* Here "awareness" refers to the nonconceptual recognition of the true nature of the three spheres. We don't fall to the extreme of affirming that everything exists as it appears, nor do we go to the other extreme of denying that anything is happening.

Because the ground of our experience consists of both relative and absolute truth, both accumulations are essential to our practice; both are indispensable for attaining enlightenment. In Vajrayana Buddhism the path is the union, or inseparability, of the two accumulations of merit and wisdom. We practice maintaining view in the midst of our daily lives, acting skillfully on a conventional level without ever losing awareness of the essential nature of our activity. This awareness is the ultimate aspect of bodhicitta, while the compassionate aspiration to benefit beings is the relative aspect.

Practice of the two accumulations leads to the realization of the two kayas: the formless aspect of enlightened mind, dharmakaya; and the expression of that ultimate realization for the benefit of others, the form kaya. Thus the ground of our experience is the union of the two truths, and our path the union of the two accumulations, which leads to the fruit: the union of the two kayas, the form and formless aspects of enlightened being.

The merit we create through our practice can be dedicated to the benefit of all beings. If you were in a dark house, the light from one butterlamp could illuminate an entire room and everyone in that room would benefit. When all the oil was burned, the light would go out. Whoever added oil to the lamp would make the light last longer, and all in the room would benefit. In a similar way, fortunate conditions in this world are the result of collective merit. Whoever creates virtue and dedicates it to all beings helps the collective merit to last longer.

Shantideva stated that just as a mountain of dry grass the size of Mount Meru can be reduced to ashes by a single spark, merit gathered over aeons that has not been dedicated can be destroyed by a single instant of anger. If we practice virtue with bodhicitta motivation and dedicate the merit to the benefit of all beings, that merit can't be destroyed. To enhance the power of our dedication, we can pray that it will be the same as that of all buddhas and bodhisattvas, who have always, and will always, dedicate their virtue to the benefit of others.

To turn the mind toward selflessness, we need to contemplate bodhicitta again and again, just as we do the four thoughts. Contemplate compassion, imagining yourself experiencing the suffering of another, then let the mind rest. Reestablish your commitment to do everything you can to relieve the suffering of beings and to help them find liberation, to awaken from the dream of suffering. Pray that, by the blessings of all sources of refuge, your aspirations will be fulfilled. Then contemplate equanimity, the equality of suffering of all beings—those who suffer in the moment and those who will suffer when their negative karma ripens. Contemplate the kindness they have all shown you, the kindness of a mother. Then let the mind relax, reestablish your commitment, pray, and so on.

If you do this throughout the day, turning for brief periods of time to each of these stages of meditation, your mind will change. Samsaric experience is like being trapped in a bag. Each time you bring the mind back to meditation, you poke a small hole in the bag. If you do this many times, it will start to shred until finally you can break free. When we bring pure motivation to everything we do, all of our activities become part of our practice.

Question: For our compassion to have an effect, shouldn't we go out into the world and do something like help the homeless?

Response: It's good to want to help in a specific way, but you must be careful, because the poisons of the mind can stain your actions. For example, you might think, "If I help the homeless, then I'm a good person." Or you might feel, "I'm a little better than the homeless because I'm providing for them." Or you might say to yourself, "I'd better help the homeless so that no one thinks I'd let people sleep on the street." If a man bites your hand when you give him a piece of bread and you get angry, or if he smiles at you and you're happy, your action is stained by pride, attachment, or aversion. These poisons can function in a very subtle manner. This is a place where many people get stuck.

Maybe you can help a thousand people, maybe even ten thousand, but they might hate you for it, or your efforts may not do any good and they'll be left as miserable as ever, no freer sleeping on a cot than on the sidewalk.

This doesn't mean we should be apathetic. We must do everything we can to relieve others' suffering in the moment. But at the same time we need to expand the sphere of our motivation, addressing the ultimate needs of all beings. It's important not to get shortsighted and focus on the human condition to the exclusion of other realms. The suffering of the homeless, while terrible, is not as great as that of beings in the hell realms. Immediate needs are different from ultimate needs. We can't be naive about this.

Before we can be truly effective in helping others, we need to develop and enhance our positive qualities. Then we won't respond to anger with anger, but with compassion. To save someone who is drowning, we need to know how to swim. Otherwise, though we mean to help, we'll only drown as well.

In short, we have to practice meditation, because it will give us the capacity to do much more for others. Eventually, we can help them on both an immediate and an ultimate level. We can't think, "I don't have time to meditate because I have to work in the soup kitchen." We have to do both simultaneously.

We have to experience personally what it is to suffer and then we can understand what suffering is for others. Otherwise, working for the sake of others becomes too theoretical. If your child fell into a deep hole and lay in terrible danger, you would do anything you could to get her out. Your heart would break until you could lift her to safety. You should feel the same about all other beings, who have been your own children, who have been your own parents.

But compassion isn't enough. If you think that you're going to help people by taking them off the sidewalk and giving them a cot, your understanding is limited. Instead, you need to probe to the root of the problem and find a way to cause both temporary and ultimate benefit. Otherwise, you can spend your whole life trying to help people but not getting anywhere. You won't find liberation, and the people you've tried to help won't either. You might make a better "dream" for yourself or others. But depending on what's at play in your mind as you act, you might not even be able to accomplish that much.

If, however, you have a pure heart, with motivation that is selfless, all-encompassing and not stained by the poisons of the mind, then even the most insignificant-seeming action can produce great merit, much more so than actions that seem only outwardly virtuous.

Motivation determines the virtue or nonvirtue produced by each action. When you offer something, for example, the merit you gather doesn't have as much to do with what you are offering as with your motivation. If you offer your most valued possession for selfish reasons, the benefit is very small. But if you offer something very small with pure motivation, the merit is enormous.

There was once a great meditator in retreat who practiced diligently day and night. One day, knowing that the sponsor of his retreat was coming to visit, he carefully cleaned his altar, water bowls, and meditation room. As he sat back down, he asked himself, "Why did I do that? My motivation wasn't pure." So he got back up and threw ashes onto the altar and throughout the room.

It might seem nonvirtuous or shameful to hit your child. But if spanking him is the only way to keep him from doing something harmful, then it is actually of great benefit.

Honesty is certainly a virtue and it's important to speak the truth, but you should do so with the proper motivation. Are you speaking the truth because you feel you're right or because you see that speaking the truth will benefit the situation? If you're speaking the truth only to prove your own point, you're simply acting out of pride.

Suppose you're in a situation where a man, looking desperate, runs past you and ducks into a doorway. A few minutes later a person with a knife comes running by and asks, "Where did he go?" Are you going to give him away, or are you going to claim you've never seen the person? What seems a negative action can actually be virtuous if it's performed for the right reason.

A bodhisattva, in this situation, would choose to lie, fully prepared to suffer the consequences. The bodhisattva wouldn't want the person to be killed or the murderer to incur the negative karma of killing.

Question: Sometimes I try so hard to do the best I can, but I don't feel that my actions have much impact.

Response: There's a story about a woman who went to a beautiful temple in Lhasa in order to pay her respects to a sacred statue of the Buddha, said to have been blessed by the Buddha himself. Being very poor, the woman possessed nothing more than a cup of turnip soup. She said to the Buddha statue, "Well, you may not like turnip soup, but this is all I've got and this is what I'm offering." It's a bit like that for us. We may not like what we have to offer, but if we do the best we can, that's all we can do.

Again, what it comes down to is motivation. There was once a man who generated great virtue by creating *tsa-tsas,* small molded forms or sculptures symbolizing enlightened mind. One day the man carefully placed one of these sculptures by the side of the road and left.

Another man came along, saw that rain was hitting the *tsa-tsa,* and thought, "How sad. It's going to get ruined." The only thing he could find for protection was the discarded sole of a shoe. So he placed this over the sculpture and left.

A third man came along, saw the sole on top of the *tsa-tsa,* and thought, "This is horrible. Someone has disrespectfully put the sole of a shoe on top of this image of enlightened mind." So he threw the sole away.

Each man had equally virtuous intentions, and the actions of each contributed toward his eventual realization of enlightened mind.

Question: Can the same action under different circumstances produce different amounts of merit?

Response: It depends on who you are directing your action

toward. For example, if you are generous to a starving, poverty-stricken, or desperate individual, that act produces significantly more merit than the same act toward an ordinary person. This is because the gratitude and rejoicing of a needy person are so much greater. There is more merit in making an offering to a spiritual practitioner than to a nonpractitioner because of the practitioner's dedication of merit. The same offering given to a practitioner with greater realization will produce even more merit because of the power of realization that is brought to the rejoicing and dedication of merit to all those with whom that practitioner has a connection.

Question: Could you talk more about the experience of connecting with our true nature?

Response: It doesn't help much to talk about it. It's better just to drop our hope and fear, rest the mind, and allow the experience of that which is beyond concepts to arise. It's not a dull or sleepy state, not like being in a coma.

The Buddha said that our true nature simply is; there are no words for it. If you have words to explain it, you're relying on concepts and you've lost it. The truth is so close, yet we don't recognize it.

It's like the horse on the first floor of a Tibetan house—we search everywhere, following hoofprints, wondering if it's here or maybe there, thinking it's this or maybe that. But it's nowhere else, it's nothing else; it's just that our concepts and the mind's poisons prevent us from recognizing it. As these are purified, we can, very simply, realize our nature directly as it is.

A person who's never tasted sugar might ask someone else what it's like. The reply will probably be, "It's very sweet." But what is "sweet"? There really is no way to explain it—you have to taste it for yourself. In the same way, the direct experience of our true nature can't be explained in words.

Question: Is there one horse in the basement or many?

Response: I'll say "many" because it's closer to the truth. If there were only one horse and only one person had it, the implication would be that others didn't have it. Yet all beings have buddha nature. However, if one person has completely realized his or her true nature, all are not enlightened. Similarly, one being might have a hellish existence, but not all beings do. So we can't really say it's just one.

But if we think there are many horses, we start seeing differences, such as big horses or small, horses so many hands high, and so on. Yet there's no way to measure the truth of our nature, for emptiness has no boundaries. In this sense you could say we're speaking of one horse.

But essentially, you can't say either that there is just one horse or that there are many. You asked a question on a relative level and I'm answering it on a relative level. But the truth is really beyond "one" and "many."

Question: You've mentioned so many different methods. How do we know which one to use and when?

Response: Our small-minded perspective creates walls around us. The walls in this room create a boundary that makes the sky outside seem different from the space inside. Yet, basically, there's no difference between them. Similarly, there is fundamentally no difference between the true nature of our body, speech, and mind and that of enlightened beings. That ultimate nature is unborn, unceasing, like the sky.

So how do we dissolve such walls? First we look at the suffering of others, generate compassion, and allow the mind to rest. Then we imagine exchanging our own fortune for others' misfortune. Then, again, we allow the mind to rest.

When we first begin meditation practice, we contemplate

the four thoughts. Then, slowly, we can incorporate into our practice an awareness of the illusory quality of our experience, which brings compassion for those who don't understand. As our view and practice deepen, we begin to recognize the true nature of these temporary appearances. The many waves that arise are not different from, but are the display of, the ocean. Without the ocean, there would be no waves. This understanding leads to a shift in perspective. It's not so much our outer experience that changes as how we see it. It's like wearing glasses with a different prescription.

If we have a fever, we take specific medicine to antidote it. If our worldly attachments prevent us from practicing diligently, we contemplate samsaric suffering and impermanence, recognizing the illusory quality of our worldly life. If our focus is on our own selfish needs and desires, we contemplate the suffering of others and generate compassion. To address the mind's duality, we allow the mind to rest. So to whatever poison or problem arises in the mind, we apply a meditational antidote.

The Buddha Shakyamuni taught 84,000 methods for cutting mind's delusion. This doesn't mean that each of us must practice every one of these. There may be hundreds or thousands of medicines in a pharmacy, but each person takes only what he or she needs. No one medicine cures all illnesses, nor will one medicine necessarily be effective through the full course of an illness. After a fever has abated, for example, one might need a new medicine to remove toxins from the system.

The important thing is to recognize that we are sick and to follow through with treatment, diligently and carefully. Then change will come inevitably.

Part IV

Introduction to Vajrayana

16 Revealing Our Foundational Nature

The 84,000 methods taught by the Buddha Shakyamuni fall into three main categories. The first, the Hinayana path, is based on the understanding that samsara is permeated by suffering and difficulty, that whatever happiness can be found is impermanent. One who follows this path makes the firm decision to practice in order to find freedom beyond suffering. By applying the methods of the Hinayana, the practitioner develops the capacity to go beyond the cycles of suffering to an experience of joyousness and bliss.

In the Mahayana, the second category, we find, in addition to this same understanding of suffering, the teaching that everything—suffering and happiness, misfortune and fortune, all of which arise as the play of karma—is illusory, like a dream, a mirage, or the reflection of the moon in water. Basic to this path is the view of the inseparability of relative and absolute truth and one's aspiration to help all beings, not only oneself, find liberation. Recognizing the great kindness shown us by all beings who have at one time been our mothers, we aspire to enlightenment in order to help them awaken to the truth of their nature. We don't just wish for this to happen, but diligently apply the methods by which enlightenment can be attained. Through the practice of the six perfections, we develop the capacity to go beyond samsara and nirvana, to find complete liberation. This is the way of the bodhisattva.

The third category of Buddhist practice is called the Vajrayana. That which is "vajra" has seven qualities: it cannot be cut by *maras,* obstacles to our enlightenment, nor grasped or separated by concepts; it cannot be destroyed by concepts which invest appearances with a truth they do not have; it is the pure truth in that there is nothing wrong within it; it is not of substance that has been compiled and can break apart; it is not impermanent, and is therefore stable and unmovable; it is unstoppable in that it is all-pervasive; and it is unconquerable in that it is more profound than everything else and thus fearless.

These are the seven qualities of our own true nature, the true nature of our body, speech, and mind. To better understand this nature, we can begin by considering that each of us has a physical body in which we experience sky and earth, friends and enemies, happiness and sadness. When this body lies down at night to sleep, even though it doesn't move from the bed, an entirely different experience of body, sky and earth, friends and enemies arises—a dream body, dream speech, and dream mind. When we wake up the next day, again we have the daytime experience of body, speech, and mind that we hold to be true. At the time of death, when the body is left behind and buried or cremated, we have another experience of body, speech, and mind in the intermediate state between the end of this life and the beginning of the next, one somewhat similar to the dream experience, but more frightening and difficult. Then, once again, we take rebirth with yet another body, speech, and mind. If we are able to completely accomplish the spiritual path, upon enlightenment we realize vajra or wisdom body, wisdom speech, and wisdom mind.

Thus there is a continuity to the principle of body, speech, and mind. Yet if, thinking it to be some "thing," we try to find it, to determine its size or shape, no matter how intelligent we may be, no matter how great the technology we may use, we won't find anything we can point to as the nature of body, speech, and mind. Yet we can't deny our own experience. This nature is beyond concept, beyond the measure of ordinary mind: what we call emptiness. It cannot be destroyed, changed, or stopped—it exhibits the seven vajra qualities. This is vajra. *Yana,* meaning "vehicle," refers to the methods by which we reveal this vajra nature.

Vajrayana practice encompasses both the Hinayana and Mahayana. On these paths of the sutras, or Buddhist scriptures, we pay careful attention to our outer actions—abandoning harmful ones and cultivating helpful ones—while taming the mind, developing and enhancing its inner qualities.

The practice of the four immeasurables, for example, is very important in the Mahayana tradition. In the Vajrayana as well, paintings of mandalas depict four doors facing the four directions, symbolizing the four immeasurable qualities. In the eastern direction lies the door of compassion, the southern direction the door of love, the western direction that of joy, and the northern direction equanimity. In the Vajrayana, the mandala is understood to be the display of mind's intrinsic purity. As our obscurations are purified, pure qualities of mind arise in the form of the mandala and the appearance of the pureland, the deity, and all pure experience. The four immeasurable qualities are doorways by which we enter the truth, the absolute nature of mind.

Further, because many different obstacles can make it difficult to maintain the purity of heart we're aspiring to, we contemplate the four thoughts—precious human birth, impermanence, karma, and suffering—which are foundational to all Buddhist practice.

On the Vajrayana path, upon the view of the absolute

nature beyond extremes, we practice virtuous and unharmful actions. Although our intrinsic nature is vajra body, speech, and mind, we don't now experience that to be true. To resolve this ignorance, we listen to and contemplate the Vajrayana teachings and then practice both effortful and effortless meditation. Although effortless meditation, simply allowing the mind to rest in its true nature, is difficult for many people at first, through effortful practice the mind's obscurations are purified, ignorance is transformed to knowing, and effortless meditation arises spontaneously. Once we recognize the absolute nature, our practice becomes that of maintaining this awareness, understanding the inseparability of form and emptiness as wisdom body, the body of the deity; of sound and emptiness as wisdom speech, the speech of the deity; and thought and emptiness as wisdom mind, the mind of the deity. With this view and the methods of the Vajrayana, we are able to reveal the inherent purity of our nature in a relatively short time.

Another name for the Vajrayana is "secret mantra path." In that our buddha nature remains concealed from us—as unenlightened beings, we're not aware of it—we refer to it as "self-secret." Also, the Vajrayana path, though extremely potent and effective, is, by its very nature, a delicate process and hence not widely taught. We maintain a certain privacy, preserving the very personal quality of working with and receiving direct transmission from a Vajrayana teacher. That is why deeper and more detailed teachings require a personal commitment from a person seeking training in Vajrayana practice.

The term "mantra" in "secret mantra path" denotes something that swiftly provides protection and shelter. Through the skillful application of the Vajrayana methods, we protect ourselves from confusion and the negative karma it produces, and can thus attain enlightenment in a single lifetime.

In the Vajrayana tradition, we must first receive empowerment to ripen the mind and create receptivity to the teachings and practice. Without empowerment, we are not authorized to listen to the teachings or to practice, for our efforts would be no more fruitful than crushing sand to make oil.

We receive the foundation empowerment from a lama who carries the practice lineage. It can't be given through words and substance alone, for just as only a king has the necessary power to enthrone the next, only a lama who carries the lineage and has accomplishment in practice can empower another. Through the power of meditation, mantra recitation, and the symbolic use of substances, we are empowered into both development and completion stage practice, and to recognition of the body, speech, and mind of the deity and of our absolute nature.

Once we have received this foundation empowerment from the lama, through our daily practice we receive the path empowerment, by which we continuously purify obscurations and enhance the pure qualities of mind in order to develop and uphold the view to which we were introduced in the foundation empowerment.

Simply receiving empowerment is not enough. The heart essence of empowerment is *samaya,* or commitment to uphold our daily practice and the vows we've taken. If we break our commitments, we will experience inauspicious circumstances in this life and great difficulties in future lives. But by keeping our samaya we will quickly find liberation.

The foundation of our being is buddha essence, buddha nature. All beings, whether large or small, have this foundational nature, this essential purity. Like gold embedded in ore, the truth of our nature, though beginningless, endless purity, isn't obvious to us. Because this is our foundational nature, we can reveal it through practice just as refinement reveals the gold inherent within ore.

This essence, from beginningless time, is completely substanceless, empty. Although we might try to find characteristics by which to define and understand emptiness, it can't be conceived by ordinary concepts. It is thus signless, or characteristicless. Nothing more is needed than to maintain recognition of our foundational nature in order for the fruit—the full qualities, the complete realization of this inherent purity—to be revealed. What we reveal is not beyond our foundational nature, and in that sense is beyond wishing. There is nothing outside, nothing elsewhere that we aspire to in order for this to happen. It is aspirationless.

Because we don't recognize this nature—we don't realize that although appearances arise unceasingly, nothing is really there—we invest with solidity and reality the seeming truth of self, other, and actions between self and others. This intellectual obscuration gives rise to attachment and aversion, followed by actions and reactions that create karma, solidify into habit, and perpetuate the cycles of suffering. This entire process is what needs to be purified.

In the first of three successive stages of teaching, referred to as the first turning of the wheel of dharma, the Buddha taught the four noble truths: the truth of suffering, its origin, the path by which it is eradicated, and its cessation. In the second turning of the wheel of dharma, he taught that the true nature of all phenomena is empty, signless, and aspirationless: the foundational nature is emptiness, the path signless, and the fruit aspirationless. In the third turning of the wheel, he spoke of the full, infallible, resplendent qualities of mind's nature, the appearance of the clear light of wisdom.

The Vajrayana tradition teaches the inseparability, from beginningless time, of these two: the union beyond words

of the unborn, absolute nature of mind and the pure qualities of the clear light of wisdom. All-pervasive, noncom-
posite, unchangeable, and pure—this is our own mind's nature. In the Vajrayana, we are introduced to these vajra
qualities of mind.

All appearances arise from the dynamic energy, or display, of our foundational nature. Experience can arise in
two ways. The reflection of the nonrecognition of our foundational nature arises as the impure experience of the three
realms of samsara. Although we may understand that our
nature is pure, this is not our ordinary experience. We
don't see, feel, or think about things in a pure way. When
we start to apply ourselves to the spiritual path, research
and probe, listen to teachings, repeatedly contemplate and
meditate on those teachings, we begin to experience a mix-
ture of pure and impure perceptions. Through spiritual
practice, we can purify obscurations and accomplish the
fruit. Our intrinsically pure foundational nature becomes
completely apparent as pure wisdom body, the full revelation of our wisdom nature, and the display of pure appearances.

Why isn't this our current experience? All ordinary
appearances of the elements—earth, fire, water, wind, flesh,
and bone—are in essence pure. But just as someone with
jaundice sees a snow mountain as yellow, due to our obscurations we don't see things purely. This impure perception has become a deeply entrenched habit. Through spiritual practice, our lack of recognition can be purified, and
then, like one cured of jaundice who can see the snow
mountain as white, we, like all the buddhas, will see the
display of purity as it is—the pure, measureless mandala of
the deity. Everything has been this way from beginningless
time. It is not something to be created, but the radiance of
the inherent qualities of our foundational nature.

This purity of our nature, unchanging throughout the

three times of past, present, and future, is now obscured, like the sun by clouds. Due to the infallible cause and effect of karma and the reflections of poisonous mind, endless appearances of environment and body arise.

Through visualization practice in the development stage of Vajrayana, we practice recognizing the pure nature and qualities of environment, body, speech, and mind as the pureland and the body, speech, and mind of the deity. This purifies the obscurations of mind that create the grosser reflections of our mind's lack of recognition: the three realms of experience and the three doors of body, speech, and mind, transforming the habit to perceive in an ordinary way.

Through the completion stage of Vajrayana practice, we purify the more subtle obscurations. The visualization we create is completely resolved into emptiness and we rest effortlessly in awareness of mind's nature.

In the Vajrayana, we recognize that all possible phenomenal appearances of samsara and nirvana, from beginningless time, are equal, without separation or distinction, within their completely pure buddha nature, like night-dream appearances within the absolute truth of the dream. Upon this view, we apply method and wisdom, development and completion stage practice, which, like medicines used to treat illness, purify the habit to hold to these temporary reflections of delusion as solid and reveal our intrinsic purity.

Through repeated application of these methods, we fully realize the fruit: like clouds swept away to reveal the unchanging sky, our obscurations resolve and beginningless purity is revealed. Our foundational nature is realized as the inseparability of the three kayas. The resplendent full qualities of dharmakaya appear as the sambhogakaya to tenth-level bodhisattvas and as the nirmanakaya to ordinary beings, creating ceaseless benefit.

Because our nature is beginningless purity, *dharmata,* we don't need to do anything to it or take anything from it, enhance or reduce it, to make it manifest. Rather, using the methods that are the path, we simply reveal it as it is. Then our lack of understanding of this nature, our mind's ordinary habits and delusions, which are reflected in the impure samsaric experience we call reality, are completely resolved into the absolute nature.

In the Vajrayana, the path isn't conceived as starting with something to which we add certain causes and conditions to arrive at something different. We use awareness of the foundational nature to reveal it as the fruit of the path. We simply remove the temporary obscurations that prevent this complete realization. By contemplating and meditating repeatedly upon this understanding, it will be easy to rely on the Vajrayana to find accomplishment.

The Vajrayana tradition includes outer, inner, and secret methods of practice. When we do outer deity practice, what, really, is the deity? In essence, the nature of dharmata, the absolute truth of our own mind and of all experience, is the absolute deity. The deity is not something we make up or create that wasn't there already, but the spontaneous display of the absolute truth, the manifestation not of anything ordinary, but of wisdom. This is the mandala of bodhicitta mind.

The nature of all beings, of all phenomena, is dharmata. Within the absolute nature there is no distinction or separation between self and other. It is all of one taste. All phenomena arise inseparably from, and are contained within, the absolute nature. None of our experience—not the elements, not phenomena, not even a single molecule— is beyond the absolute nature, nor what we call basic space. It is all-pervasive and true.

If we don't recognize this nature, we experience ourselves and all phenomena to be different from the deity.

For example, in that the night dream is all-pervasively empty nature, there is really no separation between ourselves and the land, the sky, the water. When we awaken, we see that all unceasing experiences that arose in the dream were only mind's display, empty yet appearing. But if we don't recognize that we're dreaming, in the context of the dream it all appears to be separate and true in and of itself.

Similarly, from the perspective of ordinary mind, we perceive differences between the day and night bodies, between ourselves and others, between somebody who helps us and somebody who is difficult. Yet on the level of absolute truth, nobody ever comes or goes. It is all the display of mind. If we don't know the nature of our experience, we don't know the absolute deity, then we experience ourselves as separate from the deity and this lack of recognition keeps us bound by karma and obscuration. If we realize our nature as the deity, all boundaries, like walls in space, are liberated and we realize vajra body. Knowing and maintaining recognition of our absolute nature, we are able to fully accomplish and reveal our nature as the deity.

Upon one's realization of dharmakaya, benefit is accomplished for oneself, and the ceaseless capacity to benefit others arises as the form kaya. Beings are aided in measureless ways by the qualities of great knowing, loving kindness, and spiritual energy, and by the power of great wisdom and the prayers and aspirations accumulated on the path to enlightenment. This display for the benefit of beings arises as the appearances of both peaceful and wrathful deities with their retinues—for example, the peaceful form of Manjushri with the wrathful aspect of Yamantaka, or the peaceful form of Vajrasattva with the wrathful aspect of Vajrakumara. In this pure wisdom display of the absolute nature of mind arises body, the form and color of the deity; speech, the mantra of the deity; and great mind, the inseparability of emptiness and compassion. The deity is an infallible source of benefit, capable of leading beings from samsara to enlightenment.

Because we are bound by obscurations and don't realize our nature as that of the deity, we practice this recognition by creating the visualization and reciting the mantra of the deity, making offerings and prayers. In this way we receive the blessings of those who have accomplished realization of enlightenment. This is outer deity practice.

In the category of inner deity practice, we visualize within our own body as the deity the subtle, pure central channel, within which moves the wisdom wind, or subtle energy, and which contains the even more subtle wisdom spheres called *bindus* or *t'higles*. This is the inner deity.

Although our experience of ordinary impure body, speech, and mind arises as the display of karmic wind, within the channels of our subtle body remains the mandala of the deity. By visualizing this mandala, working with the movement of the subtle winds, and reciting mantra, we reveal our own nature as the deity and absolute bodhicitta beyond extremes, unchanging great bliss which resides in the heart.

In secret deity practice we recognize that all of samsara and nirvana has always been equal within basic space beyond extremes, that there is nothing that can be made better or worse, that our mind's pure nature has always been unborn, spontaneous wisdom. With this understanding we have no need to place our hopes on an outer deity, nor is it necessary to exert effort. Through the most profound Buddhist method, called Great Perfection, we effortlessly, spontaneously attain liberation simply by abiding in recognition of the absolute nature within which everything is contained, from which all phenomena arise inseparably, like the ocean and the waves, or the sun and its rays.

Why are there so many different paths? First of all, the

Buddha taught many methods. Also, different lamas have different kinds of experience and expertise; students have differing capabilities and so require different approaches. Some feel the strongest connection to outer deity practice, others to the inner deity practice, and still others to the secret level of practice.

It might seem very easy simply to recognize and abide in recognition of the absolute deity, our own buddha essence. But in fact, because we're so mired in hope and fear, attachment and aversion, it is very hard. We have a multitude of concepts and habits, and when many different experiences arise, maintaining our recognition of their absolute nature is very difficult. That is why, when we begin Vajrayana practice, we focus on creating and dissolving the visualization; then we work with the inner practices and yogas; and gradually we approach the effortless completion stage and Great Perfection practice.

The teachings of the Buddhadharma are like a garden bursting with flowers of many colors and shapes. It isn't necessary to choose only one method, nor for any one person to try to apply them all.

If you are an angry person, it's very effective to do visualization practice using wrath to antidote and cut the anger in your own mind. In wrathful deity practice we visualize wrathful beings, manifestations of wisdom, with two, four, or many legs crushing negative beings, radiating sparks, and brandishing weapons. Those destroyed aren't outer beings, but our own poisons, our real enemies and demons. Self-clinging is embodied in Rudra, a very powerful being, the "owner" of samsara, who is suppressed by embodiments of wisdom. Throughout wrathful imagery, we see the play of an inner war: wisdom destroys anger, attachment, and ignorance. An angry person conquers and liberates his angry thoughts and negativity with the wrathful methods of maha yoga.

If you have very strong desire, rather than abandoning it, you can use it as the path, working with the channels and winds of the subtle body, as well as the source of inner heat and of bliss, training with your body's energies. Deities depicted in union with their consorts do not represent ordinary desire and male–female relationships, but rather the inseparability of emptiness and great bliss. On the level of inner union, the subtle channels of the body are male and the subtle winds or energies are female; inner heat is female and inner bliss, male. The union of the two produces not ordinary, but exhaustless bliss. Through desire, the practitioner of anu yoga connects with bliss and realizes the inseparability of great bliss and emptiness—wisdom. Through this practice, one purifies karma, accumulates merit, and reveals wisdom.

The paths of maha yoga and anu yoga involve effort, diligence and consistency. Those whose predominant mental poison is ignorance and who are lazy practice a third path, Great Perfection, or ati yoga. On this path, we rest effortlessly in subtle recognition of the nature of mind. This is called the path of effortless effort. All the teachings and levels of practice up to the Great Perfection involve ordinary concepts, ordinary intelligence, and ordinary effort. But in Great Perfection, awareness itself is the path. Great Perfection practitioners use the method of the absolute deity, their own intrinsic awareness.

Each of these three approaches purifies obscurations. Which we use depends on which poison is predominant in our mind: that is the door to practice we stand closest to. Whichever is strongest for us and most familiar becomes the means by which we chip away at all the mind's obscurations.

Through the various methods of the Vajrayana path, we bring three elements to our practice: the purification of obscurations, ripening of the mindstream, and enhancement of the mind's positive qualities. By these means we are able to swiftly purify samsaric experience and realize the fruit beyond samsara and nirvana: the three kayas, our all-completing foundational nature. Through these methods, wisdom is not born in us but rather becomes obvious, supporting and ripening our practice.

Question: I find it very hard to accept a lot of what you're saying. Could you speak to my concern? I'm sure I'm not the only one who feels this way.

Response: It's understandable if some of the teachings of Vajrayana are difficult to accept at first.

I never saw a watch until I was twenty-four years old. A friend of mine, another lama, purchased a brand new gadget from some crafty trader for an exorbitant price. The trader said, "The special thing about this watch is that whoever wears it will know exactly when they're going to die. You see these hands going around? They tell you exactly how much time you've got left." The lama had never seen a watch before, so he paid the price. Later he told me, "You know, it really seems to be true. See those little things going around? I guess they're slowly moving toward my death."

How could either of us have known? What reason had we to believe or disbelieve? I was a little skeptical, but I thought maybe it was true.

Later, when I first heard about the telephone, about people talking to one another across miles of mountains and rivers, I said, "That's impossible! Nobody can do that! You can shout long distances, but nobody can hear someone hundreds of miles away." I thought it was nonsense. Eventually, though, I encountered a telephone myself.

Then, a friend told a group of us, "There is a little box you can look into and watch people dancing and talking and moving around. It's just like real life!" You should have seen our eyes! I was sure this was a lie.

But it's all true. There really are boxes in which you can see these things. You really can talk to people miles and miles away.

People have a habit of believing what is familiar to them and refusing to believe what is new. Many in the West doubt that there are past and future existences simply because they have no personal knowledge of them. They don't remember having died and having been reborn, so they say it can't happen. Their opinion is based upon ignorance, just as much as is someone's firm belief that a television couldn't exist.

The most productive way to listen to the teachings is to keep an open mind and suspend judgment. Spiritual practice removes increasingly subtle layers of obscuration. The more we do, the more we will realize directly, through our own experience, what is true and possible.

Question: Are you saying that samsara is the pureland, and the pureland samsara? Did I get that right? Are they one and the same thing?

Response: Yes and no. Using ice as an analogy, you can say that ice is water; the nature of ice is not different from water. And yet ice has its own characteristics; as a solid, its appearance differs from that of water. Similarly, though samsara is not ultimately different from the pure realm of experience, it has its own characteristics. If we don't remove the mind's delusions, we see only those characteristics.

In general, we perceive phenomena in an ordinary way. We see them impurely—always zeroing in on the negative, always focusing on what's wrong. This is simply our habit. Through Vajrayana practice, we recognize that the true nature of samsara is the pureland, pure experience. We're not pretending that something is what it's not. It's just that we don't see it as it really is—and that's why we practice. By maintaining recognition of our true nature, we turn up the heat, take off the chill, and seemingly solid relative appearances, like ice melting, resume their natural form. In essence, we are never other than the deity, and the environment is never other than the pureland, though we don't perceive this as long as we remain subject to the chill of mind's delusion.

If the true nature of samsara were fully obvious to us, we would be enlightened—we wouldn't need to practice. Only when our temporary obscurations are removed through practice is our foundational nature revealed.

Question: How did we become so confused? Has it always been this way? Has our foundational nature always been obscured?

Response: In one way, you can say that lack of recognition of our true nature is the foundational problem. All the teachings tell us this. But your understanding will come clearer as you receive more profound teachings, such as those of the Great Perfection. Just as someone who is tightly bound with a rope can be freed by loosening the last knot, then the next, and so forth, as you practice you'll develop a deeper understanding, receive deeper teachings, and come closer to comprehending the origin of the problem.

Question: Why are mantras considered to be so powerful?

Response: "Mantra" (*ngag* in Tibetan) means "praiseworthy," for repetition enables us to accomplish our goals easily and swiftly. The effectiveness of mantras is due to four factors: first, their essential nature itself, that is, the very nature of reality, because they themselves do not deviate from emptiness, dharmakaya; second, their inherent nature on the phenomenal level of reality—they consist of sounds and syllables that arise spontaneously from the equanimity and compassion of buddhas, bodhisattvas, holders of intrinsic awareness, and advanced spiritual adepts; third, the blessings that derive from realized beings having consecrated them with their motivation and authentic prayers of aspiration, bringing their realization of the inseparability of deity and mantra to their spiritual practice; and fourth, their energy and power, in that they are able to confer spiritual accomplishment and blessings upon the mindstream of one who recites them repeatedly with faith.

Question: What is the difference between the deities we rely upon in practice and the gods and goddesses of the god realms?

Response: In Tibetan, the same word is used for both: *lha.* But the gods and goddesses of cyclic existence and the deities we meditate on are as different as gold and brass.

Meditational deities are a reflection of mind's true nature, manifesting in different forms for the benefit of beings. When we use *lha* to mean gods or goddesses in the samsaric sense, we refer to beings who, because of their positive karma and merit, experience higher rebirths in the desire realm or in the form and formless realms—increasingly subtle, more refined samsaric existence. Although positive karma can sustain some god realm beings for aeons in a state of bliss—and it is possible that such gods may exert some short-term benefit in other realms—at some point the momentum of positive karma ends and other predominant karmic patterns propel these beings into a lower rebirth.

Question: Does it matter what position we sit in when we meditate?

Response: Both development and completion stage practice are supported by correct body posture. When the spine is straight, the subtle channels of the body are straight and the subtle energies can move without hindrance. This helps to make the mind clear and to keep it from jumping to outer or inner objects of attention rather than resting in awareness. By sitting in posture rather than in ordinary ways, we create virtue and purify the body's obscurations. Recitation of mantra and prayers purifies nonvirtuous speech and enhances pure speech qualities. Through contemplation and other relative methods, as well as maintaining awareness of our absolute nature, we purify mind's obscurations and enhance our wisdom qualities. If we apply the three doors of body, speech, and mind simultaneously while listening to teachings and doing practice, we will quickly purify karma and accumulate both merit and wisdom.

Question: There is so much to learn, understand, and contemplate in Vajrayana Buddhism. Why is it so complicated? Is it necessary to do all these complicated things?

Response: We need a complicated method to antidote our complicated minds, which are filled with concepts and doubts. To put it another way, we need a medicine as complicated as our illness. With Vajrayana methods we cut through our habits, purify obscurations, and accumulate merit simultaneously.

Which practice you do depends on how you want to travel the spiritual path. If you live in California and want to go to New York, a bicycle can get you there. It's simple to make, simple to operate, and simple to repair. But if you want to go more rapidly, you can take an automobile. It's more complicated to make, to operate, and to repair, but it will get you there faster. Of course, you can also take an airplane, which is even more complicated to make, operate, and repair but which will get you there very quickly.

The Vajrayana is a complex path with many methods

for removing confusion and delusion, but it's also called the lightning path because it's so swift and direct. If you follow this path diligently, you can attain enlightenment in one lifetime or less.

17 Faith

Once there was an old man, a shepherd, who went each summer with his family to a special mountaintop to raise sheep and yaks. Many people passed his family's tent, and the shepherd always asked where they were traveling. They invariably replied, "We're going to see Dodrup Chen Rinpoche and receive the direct transmission of the three verses."

One year, the old man decided that he might as well go to see the lama too. He asked one family passing by if he could join them, and they agreed to let him come. So he went off, leaving all his sheep and yaks behind.

When they arrived at the lama's home, the old man, not knowing what to do and having nothing to ask of the lama, went to the kitchen, was given some food, and waited there. Meanwhile, the family requested and received a short teaching from the lama, then left for home.

The old man stayed on for one, two, then three years, helping out in the kitchen and receiving food in return, becoming like a family member to the kitchen workers. During the entire time, he never met the lama.

One day, when some visitors came, the cooks asked the old man to take tea to the lama. For the first time, he entered the master's room. When the lama saw him, he exclaimed, "Atsi! Atsi! Na kha ru rakshai treng wa dra shig yin!" which means, "Oh, my! Oh, my! Your nose is like a rudraksha bead!" Indeed, the old man's nose was very large and rough.

The old man thought to himself, "That's it, I've finally received the three-verse transmission from the lama!" He returned to his village, chanting day and night, "Atsi! Atsi! Na kha ru rakshai treng wa dra shig yin," counting the recitations on his prayer beads. The village people had great faith in him because, after all, he'd stayed with the lama for three years. They thought he must surely have extraordinary qualities by now. Whenever they became sick, had swelling or pain, they went to him. He blew on the affected area and they were cured. He became quite famous throughout the region.

One day Dodrup Chen Rinpoche developed a boil in his throat which grew to such a size that he almost choked to death. Many doctors tried to treat him, but nothing was effective. Somebody who was visiting from the old man's area told the lama, "One of your students lives near us. He can cure you."

"Who is he?" asked the lama.

"An old man who stayed with you for three years."

"I don't remember him, but tell him to come help me."

Immediately they sent someone to fetch the old man. "You must come right away," he was told, "the lama needs help."

The old man said, "The lama gave me the three-verse transmission. I will try to help him."

Before the old man arrived, a very good cushion was brought for him to sit on, a sign of great respect. As soon as he entered the room, the lama saw his nose and remembered him, thinking, "How could this one ever heal me?"

Slowly, with one-pointed concentration, the old man began to chant, "Atsi, atsi. . . ." The lama burst out laughing, the boil broke open, and he was cured.

From the Vajrayana point of view, true and lasting faith has three elements. The first we might term "spiritual awe." This is what we experience if we are naturally inspired by hearing the dharma. Something about it makes our hair stand on end. Or it's what we feel when we meet a certain teacher, enter a shrine, see an image of the Buddha or hear about his life. We experience a state of mind that is significantly different from our ordinary feelings of pleasure or happiness.

There was a great Indian scholar of the Shaivite tradition who had a masterful intellect and wrote many philosophical treatises. At one point he went to the Himalayas, and there he had a vision of the Hindu god Shiva invoking and honoring the Buddha. This made a great impression on him. Later he adopted the Buddhist religion and wrote one of the most famous prayers that the Tibetan tradition received from India, a prayer extolling the virtues of enlightenment as embodied in the Buddha Shakyamuni. Until that visionary experience, this scholar had no faith in Buddhism. It took something deeper than intellect.

Such faith is not something we can talk ourselves—or anyone else—into. Whether we have it depends not on our intellectual sophistication but on our karma. That's why we can't persuade someone to believe in the Buddhist teachings unless some karmic basis for the belief exists. One aspect of the precious human birth is having this sort of karmic predisposition toward faith and confidence in the dharma.

Although this first element of faith is not unshakable, at least it inspires us to examine the experience of suffering, its causes and how they can be eliminated, to probe the experience of happiness, its causes and how they can be cultivated, to yearn for release or liberation. The more we hear and apply the teachings, the more they resonate with our

experience, the more we appreciate their truth and are inspired to probe even more deeply, to find a teacher and follow the spiritual path. This is the second element of faith,
the faith of yearning, of longing to move toward the ultimate goal.

As the mind gradually opens, the teachings start to make
more sense and we begin to feel a connection with meditation. We have to have enough trust to follow through with
our practice, and when it begins to create changes within
us, that trust deepens. The mind begins to relax and we
start to experience faith in and commitment to a purpose
beyond changing, grinding reality. With that faith, our enthusiasm grows even more. And with more practice, we discover an uncompromising diligence. Practice reveals truth;
truth liberates the poisons of the mind, freeing us to greater
and greater wisdom. Each step is linked to the next. Finally
we acquire a trust that's invincible. No matter what happens to us, no matter what our plight, unshakable faith upholds our practice until we find complete freedom: enlightenment. This is the third aspect of faith, the conviction that
we have thoroughly and profoundly understood an infallible
truth. Such faith is incontrovertible.

The first element of faith, awe, is something more or
less inborn. You either feel it or you don't. The second
two—longing and conviction—arise from practice and can
be consciously increased. Thus, in the Vajrayana tradition,
we aren't expected or even encouraged to have blind faith.
True faith arises when we have heard the teachings, applied
them, and assimilated them until we experience the infallible truth.

What we have faith in now is samsara—whatever we experience of the world through our senses. But putting our
trust in such things won't help us in the long run because
they're all impermanent. We rely on our body, for example,

but eventually it will die. We depend on outer conditions, but they are always changing. We have trust in our friends, but friends may sour or drift away. Once we reveal our unchanging nature, that indeed becomes something on which we can confidently rely.

Suppose you have some new friends who immediately think you're the most wonderful person in the world. Such friends may last about a week. Or there is something they want from you, and they're not really your friends at all, just good actors. On the other hand, you may have friends who aren't so easy to please at first. They don't fall all over you or smile their biggest smile when they see you. But slowly, as you get to know them, you see that they are strong and true: they follow through.

Having faith in samsara is like depending on a flashy friendship, one that is immediate but impermanent. To place faith in the ultimate truth is to trust what's not obvious to begin with, what at first may seem elusive, intangible, and inaccessible. Yet in the long run, this is the truest, strongest object of trust. The spiritual path is not easy, for it forces us to confront just about everything we ever thought of as true or real. But if we follow through, this path will prove itself a supremely dependable friend.

18 Prayer

Why do we pray? We might think that if we do the Buddha, or God, or the deity will look kindly upon us, bestow blessings, protect us. We might believe that if we don't, the deity won't like us, might even punish us. But the purpose of prayer is not to win the approval or avert the wrath of an exterior God.

To the extent that we understand Buddha, God, the deity to be an expression of ultimate reality, to that extent we receive blessings when we pray. To the extent that we have faith in the boundless qualities of the deity's love and compassion, to that extent we receive the blessings of those qualities.

Sometimes we project human characteristics onto things that aren't human. For example, if we sentimentally think, "My dog is meditating with me," we're only attributing that behavior to the dog; we're imagining what it's doing. When we anthropomorphize God, we project our own faults and limitations, imagining they're God's as well. This is why many people believe that God either likes or dislikes them depending on their behavior. "I won't be able to have this or that because God doesn't like me—I forgot to pray." Or worse, "If God doesn't like me, I'll end up in hell."

If God feels happy or sad because we do or do not offer prayer, then God is not flawless, not an embodiment of perfect compassion and love. Any manifestation of the absolute truth, by its very nature, has neither attachment to our prayers nor aversion to our lack of them. Such attributes are projections of our own minds.

To understand how prayer works, consider the sun, which shines everywhere without hesitation or hindrance. Like God or Buddha, it continuously radiates all its power, warmth, and light without differentiation. When the earth turns, it appears to us that the sun no longer shines. But that has nothing to do with the sun; it's due to our own position on the shadow side of the earth. If we inhabit a deep, dark mine shaft, it's not the sun's fault that we feel cold. Or if we live on the earth's surface but keep our eyes closed, it's not the sun's fault that we don't see light. The sun's blessings are all-pervasive, whether we are open to them or not. Through prayer, we come out of the mine shaft, open our eyes, become receptive to enlightened presence, the omnipresent love and compassion that exist for all beings.

Even if we aren't familiar with the idea of praying to a deity, most of us feel the presence of some higher principle or truth—some source of wisdom, compassion, and power with the ability to benefit. Praying to that higher principle will without doubt be fruitful.

However, it is very important not to be small-minded in prayer. You might want to pray for a new car, but how do you know if a new car is what you need? It's better simply to pray for what's best, realizing that you may not know what that is. A few years ago, a Tibetan woman traveled overseas by airplane. When the plane made a brief stop en route, she got out to walk around. Unfamiliar with the airport, with the language, and with foreign travel, she didn't hear the announcement of her departing flight and missed it. This probably seemed disastrous at the time, but not long after take-off the plane she missed crashed, killing most of the passengers.

We pray for what's best not only for ourselves, but for all beings. When we're just starting practice, our self-importance is often so strong that our prayers remain very selfish and only reinforce rather than transform self-centeredness. So until our motivation becomes more pure-hearted, it may be beneficial to spend more time cultivating loving kindness than praying.

With proper motivation, prayer becomes an important component of our practice because it helps to remove obstacles—counterproductive circumstances, imbalances of the subtle energies in the body, confusion and ignorance in the mind. Even in listening to the teachings, we may mentally edit what we hear, adding more to them than is being said or ignoring certain aspects. Prayer offsets these hindrances.

The mind is like a mirror. Although our true nature is the deity, what we now experience are ordinary mind's reflections. Enemies, hindrances, inauspicious moments—all of which appear to be outside of us—are actually reflections of our own negativities. If you'd never seen your image before, looking in a mirror you'd think you were gazing through a window, encountering someone altogether independent of you. It wouldn't seem to have any connection to you as you passed by. If you saw there a horrible-looking person with a dirty face and wild hair, you might feel aversion. You might even try to clean up the image by washing the mirror. But a mirror, like the mind, is reflective—it only shows you yourself. Only if you combed your hair and washed your face could you change what you saw. You'd have to change yourself; you couldn't change the mirror. Prayer helps to purify the habits of ordinary, small mind and ignorance of our true nature as the deity.

When we pray in the context of deity practice, we sometimes visualize the deity standing or sitting before us in

space as an embodiment of perfection, whereas we ourselves have many faults and obscurations. But praying to
the deity is not a matter of supplicating something separate
from ourselves. The point of using a dualistic method, visualizing the deity outside of us, is to eliminate duality.

In prayer, we visualize our inherent purity reflected as
the deity, and our positive qualities as the deity's form,
color, and implements. This helps us remember what already exists at the source: our perfect nature. When we visualize ourselves as the deity, we deepen our experience of
our own intrinsic purity. Finally, in the completion stage of
practice, when the form of the deity falls away, we let the
mind rest, without effort or contrivance, in its own nature,
the ultimate deity.

Thus we begin with an initial conception of purity as
external, only to internalize it and ultimately to transcend
concepts of inner and outer. This awareness of the nature
of the deity increases the power, blessings, and benefit of
our prayer.

If the nature of the deity is emptiness, you might wonder why we pray at all. There seems to be a contradiction
here. How can we say, on the one hand, that there isn't a
deity, only the reflection of our own intrinsic nature, and,
on the other, that we should pray to it? This makes sense
only if we understand the inseparability of absolute and
relative truth.

On the absolute level, our nature is buddha, we are the
deity. But unaware of this, we're bound by relative truth. In
order to make the leap to the realization of our absolute nature, we have to walk on our relative feet, on a relative
path. Because absolute truth is so elusive to our ordinary,
linear mind, we rely on an increasingly subtle, step-by-step
process to work with mind's duality until we achieve recognition. Prayer is an essential part of that process.

19 Conversation with a Student

Student: If the ultimate nature of experience is emptiness, what, really, is karma? Isn't it just a concept that's as illusory as any other?

Rinpoche: What's involved here is the difference between absolute and relative truth. If you're not sleeping, there's no truth to the dream. Good or bad, like or dislike, sad or happy—none of it has any validity. Karma's not there at all, because the dream isn't there.

But when you're dreaming, there is good and bad, like and dislike, sad and happy, all of which create karma. If the mind is in a state of delusion, in the dream experience of relative reality, then karma is true and will make the dream better or worse. But when you awaken to the ultimate reality, there is no truth to karma, no truth to merit, no truth to any of it, any more than there is truth to the dream once you've awakened.

Awake, you have the *capacity* to dream—but you're not dreaming. It's the same with absolute truth. Relative truth is one's deluded experience of absolute truth, and within that, karma remains very powerful, merciless, accurate, and complete. Karma will determine whether we have a pleasant or an unpleasant existence, whether our rebirths are happy or sad, high or low.

Student: Is it the same with the concept of merit?

Rinpoche: Merit functions by the same process as karma, except that it involves actively working toward creating the causes of happiness in the dream of life, not only for oneself but for others.

Student: With karma and merit, the same principle seems to apply: that what I put out will come back to me. This seems to imply self-centered motivation, the opposite of bodhicitta intention. But isn't it purer for a practitioner simply to remain compassionate without regard for the good karma being generated, in other words, without concern for his or her ultimate "reward"?

Rinpoche: You're right when you say that having compassion is better than having the ambition to make good karma so that you don't suffer. The latter is true, but it's also relative. The teachings have different levels, and people's receptivity or perceptivity determines the most appropriate level of teaching for them. For some, a subtle seed may be planted in the mind. For others, a somewhat grosser seed must come first, to make them ready for the subtle seed.

So regarding self-centered motivation versus the decision to simply be compassionate, it's true—the latter remains the ultimate choice.

Student: In terms of practice, then, does merit come down to compassion in all things? Is this the essence of bodhicitta intention?

Rinpoche: Compassion is only part of bodhicitta. The difference between bodhicitta and no bodhicitta depends on whether one has the aspiration to attain enlightenment for the benefit of others. Even if you act as if you're trying to benefit others, even if it looks good outwardly, if your heart isn't really in the attainment of enlightenment for others' benefit, then it isn't bodhicitta. Compassion is the impulse, and then upon that impulse, you do whatever needs to be done. You aspire to attain enlightenment because you realize that you don't have the power to be of much benefit now.

Recognizing the suffering of beings in samsara, generating pure thoughts and compassion, developing the wish to attain enlightenment to liberate beings, and doing everything you can to benefit others temporarily and ultimately— all of that is relative bodhicitta. It's all activity within the dream that leads toward waking up from the dream. Absolute bodhicitta means recognizing the absolute truth beyond extremes and maintaining that recognition until it is fully obvious. That's when we awaken from the dream.

Student: If the ultimate nature of reality is buddhahood, shared by all beings, why doesn't everyone realize this already? What has caused the lapse into ignorance and obscuration? Is there an evolutionary principle involved here, beginning in ignorance and ideally moving on to higher consciousness?

Rinpoche: It's not a matter of having had it once and forgotten it. Inherent within raw ore is gold, though it's not apparent because it's embedded in the ore. Extracting the gold requires a smelting process. The impurities are refined away until all that's left is the gold in its pure essence. Basically, that's what one does as a practitioner. One removes all the impurities to reveal what is, in essence, there. It wasn't once realized and then forgotten. It's always been there, but never actualized.

The difference between buddhahood and deluded samsaric continuance lies in recognition or nonrecognition of one's true nature. The essence is either known or not known. That's the only difference. It isn't a matter of evolution. Samsara is not an evolutionary process. Delusion is not evolutionary. Realization happens through the revelation of something inherent.

Student: So the idea of a person's consciousness evolving over lifetimes is illusory?

Rinpoche: Yes. Consciousness does not evolve over lifetimes. We're in the midst of the flow of samsaric continuance. But as humans, we have the peak opportunity for attaining buddhahood.

Student: Why is that?

Rinpoche: Because there is not as much false contentment in the human realm as in the god realms, nor as much suffering as in the lower realms. Our conditions are neither too good nor too bad, and that's very conducive to liberation. But samsara isn't an evolutionary process, and achieving enlightenment isn't either. Once a person is able to see through samsara, that realization never goes away. On that basis, we walk the bodhisattva path.

I suppose in a sense you could consider the bodhisattva path evolutionary, since it involves relative progress toward buddhahood. But it's more like evolving inwardly toward realization of one's true nature, having gone so far out into delusion. What evolution forgets to take into consideration is de-evolution. Every sentient being goes both up and down. The process is cyclical, not evolutionary. The evolutionary theory has a lot of hope in it, but in samsara there is not much hope.

Student: Then ultimately our perception of time as linear is an illusion?

Rinpoche: Again, it's like a dream. If the mind is in the relative dream context, time exists. If the mind awakens to the absolute truth, time is nonexistent. But dream after dream, samsaric experience continues to cycle.

Student: How does the practitioner know if a particular visualization is not just more of the same noisy mental activity, but rather transcends it?

It's as if the practice consists of looking out a full-length window and painting what you see on a canvas; you re-create the scene, and when you're done you wipe it away. What is the difference between looking out the window while re-creating it on the canvas, and opening the window and walking out? In other words, when does practice become realization?

Rinpoche: Suppose a person sees a rope on the floor but thinks it's a snake; his reaction will be based on his belief that it is a snake. Though it isn't really true, his perception of what is true can even affect those around him. Suddenly, they all think the same thing. The rope becomes so real as a snake that it seems to slither around. The fear, the reaction, the whole framework of the delusion is blown into a full picture. But if someone comes along and says, "That's not a snake," everyone is greatly relieved. The lie has been exposed. They can see the rope as it is, as it always has been. Their delusion manipulated their perception. Those with very strong habits might see a snake again the next time they look, even though they've been told otherwise.

It's because of our tendency to fall back into old habits that we use visualization; we purify distorted perceptions by visualizing phenomena purely, as the deity and the pureland. We learn how to see the snake differently until finally we can see that it really is a rope.

A few extremely fortunate beings with very subtle capacities don't have to practice visualization. They're freed immediately upon being introduced to the nature of mind. Their delusion is like a cloud blown away by the wind. When it's gone, it's gone; it doesn't manifest again. Their practice then simply involves abiding in recognition of their true nature.

We take two different tacks in order to attain realization. One involves visualization practice, because our habits lie very deep. Even though we are introduced to our ultimate nature, our initial recognition doesn't stick. Visualization is a process of unlearning what we have learned and untying the knots of our ignorance. But if we don't need that process, we take the other tack and go directly to the highest path, the Great Perfection, simply resting in nondual awareness as all delusion blows away. Pure phenomena are revealed as the display of one's absolute nature. The Great Perfection practitioner never has to draw on the canvas but walks directly out the window.

Student: So emptiness emanates as appearances of the deities?

Rinpoche: All form is the deity; all form is in essence emptiness arising as appearance. The deity isn't only a being sitting on a lotus; the deity is emptiness arising as form. This means that everything in our world, including our enemies, is the deity. When someone tries to hurt us, it's hard for us to remember that, so we revert to old habits. That's why we use visualization. It's a relative method for awakening to absolute truth, but absolute truth actually appears in the form of this relative method.

Comprehending more fully what we talked about earlier —the difference between absolute and relative truth, and the workings of karma within relative truth—will help you to understand more about visualization.

Student: And, as a consequence, the movement toward realization?

Rinpoche: Realization is not a grandiose type of thing. Rather, it is like penetrating something to sense or taste its essence. It's the difference between talking about what sweet means and experiencing sugar on your tongue. Realization is a manner of experiencing, of tasting. Meditation is the path of continuing, of keeping at it, of allowing a transformative alchemy to occur.

There are four parts to the process. First as you begin to wonder about reality, to question what's true and what's not, you see that many people just accept phenomenal reality at face value. When you realize this, you feel compassion for them. Out of compassion, you pray to the lama. The lama is the source of your realization, the source of your practice. Realization has no limitations, so there is no separation between the lama and the deity. As you mature in your practice, your understanding of the lama will mature. The lama is the deity; the lama is the truth.

You pray to the lama for clarity, strength of practice, inspiration, motivation, whatever you need under the lama's umbrella of blessing. Then you do your visualization. If it's hard, if it doesn't work, or if it makes you grumpy, just drop it and relax. Let the mind be as the mind is. Then, when thoughts resurface, try visualization again. If you find it difficult to envision all the details, just focus on one aspect of the visualization or on your own form as an intangible, luminous body of light. Or just imagine that the deity in front of you is, in essence, the embodiment of compassion and wisdom, the absolute truth.

Don't be too hard on yourself. When you can't visualize, remind yourself that you have very strong habits that make you see reality as you do. Accept your difficulties, and then just go on. Every time there's a pothole, don't let it stop you. Just go around it, or jump over it. A good practitioner is indomitable. Say to yourself, "Of course I have faults, of course I have shortcomings, of course I'm impatient, of course I'm lazy." But then go on. Take little steps, big steps—it doesn't matter, as long as you go forward.

20 Preparing for Death

Death awaits us all, whether or not we're prepared, whether or not we choose to think about it. For many of us the thought of dying engenders such uneasiness that we prefer to avoid it completely. We might even fool ourselves into believing we're not afraid of death, that it's not such a big deal. But those who die without preparation are gripped by tremendous fear, a fear that can't be compared to anything they've ever experienced. The lack of power over the body, the loss of everything familiar brings not only terror, but disorientation and confusion. Some people feel great regret, a sense that their lives, all their efforts, have been without purpose. They feel a tremendous sadness in looking back and discovering they've missed the point of it all.

We need to prepare for the moment when the mind and body separate by developing strong habits of spiritual practice that won't evaporate in the face of death. There is a Tibetan saying: once you're caught short, it's too late to build the latrine. If we become familiar with the process of dying, we won't be taken by surprise; we won't be paralyzed by fear or distracted by confusion. If we develop the necessary meditative skill, death can be a door to the deathless state of enlightenment whereby we ceaselessly benefit all beings.

When the elements that comprise the physical body remain in balance, we stay healthy. The earth element relates to flesh and bones, the water element to blood and other

174

bodily fluids, the fire element to digestion and heat, and the different winds to the breath, circulation, and the binding of mind to body. If the balance of elements is tipped, however, and one becomes more dominant than another, we fall ill. We might find signs of approaching death in our dreams. Dreaming of being naked, headed in a southerly direction, riding an ox or a donkey, following the setting sun, veering downward, or repeatedly meeting and talking with those who have already died—all indicate some weakening of the life force.

Vajrayana practice, especially long-life practice, can be very effective for purifying the karma that causes illness and for accumulating merit—creating the positive conditions necessary to prolong life. If you aren't familiar with such meditation, you can generate great merit by saving animals that would otherwise be killed. For example, you might buy all the fresh fish and worms in a bait shop and set them free, motivated by the compassionate understanding that no being wants to die, that each values its existence, and that great virtue comes from saving a life. Dedicate the virtue you create to all who are experiencing obstacles to long life and pray that these obstacles will be removed. Do this repeatedly. If your dream signs don't change, it means that the karma sustaining your life is coming to an end, that death is not far away.

When you are seriously ill, the sense faculties begin to fail. Unless you are familiar with your mind's true nature, this will be a very frightening and confusing time, for all you have ever relied upon to orient yourself falls away. Your vision becomes cloudy, appearances seem mirage-like and unstable, visionary experiences may arise. Your body feels heavy, as if it were sinking into the bed.

At death, the elements lose their power. They no longer support one another, and the mind separates from the body. When the elements begin to disassociate, the ability to conceptualize, to differentiate between self and other, subject and object, diminishes. The male energy stored in the crown of the head descends, the female energy in the navel rises, and the two join in the heart. You fall into a death swoon, a coma-like state you don't come back from. At that point, all poisonous thoughts cease and the mind opens to an experience of the clear light; this is the first phase of the *chhönyid bardo,* the bardo of the true nature of reality.

The term "clear light" doesn't refer to a big light in the sky or what people who have had near-death experiences describe: a brilliant light to which they are drawn closer and closer, a voice saying, "You have to go back now." Clear light doesn't have anything to do with light per se; it indicates clarity in the sense of absence of delusion, of object–subject duality, dullness, and concepts. It refers to open awareness and is also called *foundational clear light* because it is the foundational nature of all beings.

If we are skilled in resting in awareness of our mind's nature, we can find liberation in the *chhönyid* bardo by recognizing the clear light as our own inherent nature. This blending of awareness with the clear light produces *dharmakaya liberation.*

If we don't have meditative accomplishment, the clear light arises like a flash of lightning, and is gone. Unfamiliar with the true nature of mind, we are unable to use this brief transition to attain enlightenment.

Next the reflections of mind begin to arise as a pure display of colors and deities; this is the second phase of the *chhönyid* bardo. If we recognize these phenomena as none other than the radiance of our intrinsic awareness, this transition becomes an opportunity to attain liberation, called *sambhogakaya liberation.* If, however, we have no understanding of how the mind projects appearance, we won't recognize this display for what it is. It will be like momentarily catching sight of our shadow but not recognizing it.

If our practice of the Great Perfection paths of *t'hregchhod* and *t'hodgal* has been strong, we can find liberation in one of these two phases of the *chhönyid* bardo. Otherwise, these opportunities for liberation elude us, and the mind's duality takes form as the experience of self and other, the process of ordinary sentience in samsaric reality. We enter the *sidpa bardo,* or bardo of becoming, the forty-nine-day transition to rebirth. At that time, our consciousness, unfettered by the physical body, is buffeted about, encountering frightening sights and terrifying sounds. Any arising thought instantaneously propels us to its object. If in life we developed a strong habit of praying when things seemed beyond hope, we will remember to pray at this time. The moment we think of our source of refuge, we will be reborn in that wisdom being's pure realm. This is called *nirmanakaya liberation.*

If not, the mind will move into another dream, taking rebirth in one of the six realms, with all of the opportunities to awaken, to find rebirth beyond suffering, lost.

A method termed *p'howa* can be used at the moment of death to transfer one's consciousness to a pureland. Unlike a god realm, a pureland is the display of one's inherent purity, a realm of infinite bliss beyond samsara. Those who have attained such rebirth know no suffering and eventually attain enlightenment.

Called the *meditation of nonmeditation* because it is relatively easy to accomplish, *p'howa* is widely taught in the Vajrayana tradition even to beginners, for it provides safety at the time of death. After very little practice, signs of accomplishment appear, indicating that the channels of the subtle body are no longer blocked and that one's consciousness will easily transfer through the crown of the head to a pure realm of experience at death. This practice is like a bridge linking dharma from this life to the next.

Some Vajrayana practitioners don't need to rely on formal transference of consciousness practice because of the strength of their development and completion stage meditation. During the dissolution of the development stage, we visualize the entire universe—all the elements—resolving into the seed syllable of the deity, which itself disappears into emptiness. Then we abide in the nature of mind. This is completion stage. Finally, once again we recognize all form, sound, and thought as the body, speech, and mind of the deity. The practice of maintaining this awareness of vajra body, speech, and mind consistently throughout our lives can produce liberation in the bardo.

If you are dying and aren't familiar with Vajrayana or don't have confidence in your practice, visualize that whoever you have enduring faith in—your lama if you're a practitioner—is inseparable from the Buddha Amitabha, surrounded by his retinue in the pureland, resting a forearm's length above the crown of your head. Every day until you die, before the Buddha Amitabha as your witness, confess and purify all of the nonvirtue you've committed in this and all previous lives. Dedicate all of the virtue you've accumulated to the benefit of all beings and pray that at the time of death, without any other rebirth intervening, you and all beings will find rebirth in Amitabha's pureland, Dewachen, receive teachings directly from Amitabha, practice, and attain enlightenment, the capacity to benefit all beings. Normally, the pure realm of experience is revealed when all the obscurations that mask our inherent purity have been removed. Because impure perceptions will make it difficult to achieve a pure experience at death, we focus on the Buddha Amitabha as the expression of flawless purity. Even if visualization is difficult, Amitabha's commitment is that whoever hears his name or prays to him, no matter how nonvirtuous, will eventually find rebirth in his pureland.

If you aren't a practicing Buddhist or if you're not familiar with the Buddha Amitabha's appearance, you can focus on the space above the crown of your head. There are two benefits to doing this. First, by focusing elsewhere, you distract yourself from your pain and fear. Second, your consciousness leaves the physical body through any one of nine "doors," each leading to a different rebirth. Eight fingers back from the original hairline, at the crown of your head, lies the door to rebirth in the pureland. In the days before you die and at the time of death, focus there, visualizing your mind merging with space. Even if you don't achieve rebirth in the pureland, you will not be born in a lower realm.

If you yourself are helping a dying person—someone of a different faith—you can describe this visualization practice. But you will only create confusion and make things more difficult if, when death is imminent, you start talking in Buddhist terms. Instead, support the person by suggesting that she visualize the object of her faith above the crown, praying at death to join that wisdom being in heaven or whatever she considers to be a pure realm. At the moment of death, tap the crown of her head. This will bring the consciousness to the door leading to the pureland. Don't touch any other part of the body, for that will draw the consciousness to a lower door, possibly a lower rebirth.

It's very helpful to encourage relatives and loved ones to leave before the moment of death. They should say what they wish and then bid their goodbyes. Otherwise, their attachment to the dying person or her attachment to them might prove distracting, and instead of concentrating on the visualization of the source of refuge or the space above the crown, she will focus on them.

If, before they die, people don't let go of their attachments to the ones they love and the objects they cherish, their minds may be caught by these attachments after death and they may become what we call ghosts. And though it is not their intention to harm, their consciousness will hover in the human realm and be felt by those they've left behind, who may experience discomfort or illness. Focusing on the light, the Buddha Amitabha, or other source of refuge above the crown helps to draw attention away from such attachments.

No matter what your age, it's very important that you write a will. If you die without one, you may still cling to your possessions, possibly leading to rebirth as a hungry ghost. You will also miss the benefit of having given your things away; you won't have created nonvirtue in your death, yet you won't have produced any virtue either. Offering your belongings to others is an act of generosity that generates virtue.

In addition to providing for the support of your family and children in your will, you can also leave something to those who are hungry or sick, or to practitioners. In Buddhism, there is a tradition that may exist in other religions as well: that of making offerings to monasteries on behalf of those who are sick or who have died. During daily services, prayers are offered for the benefit of all those who, since its founding, have had a connection to the monastery through their faith, prayers, and offerings of effort, substance, or financial support. All of this merit is continuously dedicated, producing great multiplication of virtue and long-term benefit. If you leave a donation to a monastery or church in your will, before you die dedicate the virtue of your offering, and the benefit it will produce, to all beings.

If you haven't prepared a will, even if you can no longer speak or write you can formulate a dedication in your mind: "To whomever needs or wants it, I give everything I've accumulated in order to benefit all beings." This act of generosity, too, will create virtue.

It's crucial to begin preparing for death now, whether you're young or old, healthy or sick. Begin by reflecting on impermanence. Each night when you go to bed, remember that this day may have been your last—you may not awaken in the morning. Then review your life and think about its purpose. Reflect on the fact that death is the greatest of all transitions. Visualizing the Buddha Amitabha or the wisdom being in whom you have faith, recall the nonvirtue you've created and purify your wrongdoings by invoking the four powers: the power of support, regret, commitment, and blessing. Also reflect on the practice you've done and the ways you've been helpful, and dedicate this virtue to every being. If you haven't yet bequeathed your worldly possessions, mentally give them away to whomever might need them. Don't cling to anything. Then dedicate this virtue to every being with the wish that samsaric suffering will cease, that all might awaken to their true nature. Pray that you and others will go directly—without any other rebirth intervening—to the pureland. Or if you're not a Buddhist, pray that you and all beings after death will attain whatever state you believe lies beyond painful existence.

Then imagine your death. Imagine a car wreck, a heart attack, or the misery of cancer. Imagine how it would feel to be carried away in an ambulance, hearing the doctor say, "There's nothing to be done now." Fear and an overwhelming feeling of helplessness will arise. You will experience attachment to your family, sense the futility of your life, feel the suffering of impending death. At that point, say to yourself, "I'm dying. Clinging to my family or my money won't give me one second more. But everyone dies. The greatest spiritual masters and most powerful beings down to the tiniest insects have come and gone. Death is a transition, just as is this dreamlike experience called life. I've undergone both many times before. Now, at least, I have methods that will help me. Most other beings aren't so fortunate. This time death is an opportunity for liberation." Repeated contemplation such as this can give rise to great inspiration and rejoicing.

Before you go to sleep, clearly imagine your object of faith above your head. Pray that by the power of your accumulated virtue and the blessings of your source of refuge, you and every other being will upon death attain rebirth in a pure realm. Then visualize your consciousness moving out through the crown of your head to join inseparably with the heart essence of the wisdom being above or with basic space.

Such preparation not only helps to reduce fear and anguish and increase your meditative capacity at the time of death, it also strengthens your understanding of the preciousness of this human opportunity and reinforces your aspiration to use whatever time remains to the greatest benefit for yourself and others. You can complete this nightly contemplation by praying, "If I don't die tonight, if I awaken tomorrow, I will commit myself to using my body, speech, and mind fully to practice and bring benefit." Even if half or three-quarters of your life has passed and you haven't yet placed much emphasis on this commitment, you can still do so now.

Many people think that, if they prepare for death, they'll invite it. Yet poor people are always dreaming about becoming rich, and hungry people about food, and that doesn't make them rich or fill their stomachs. No matter how much we might imagine living for a long time, we still may die young. It's not true that by focusing on our death we hasten it.

Throughout the day, remind yourself that death isn't far away. All it takes is a small blood clot lodging in your brain or a car running a red light. Although pondering this may be uncomfortable, the more you do it, the more it will help to reduce your fear.

At the time of death our consciousness revisits all the places we've ever been. If, when alive, wherever you go, you practice praying to the lama, to the deity, or to some other source of refuge that you and all beings might find rebirth in the pureland, then when your consciousness returns to these places at death, your memory of having prayed there will lead you to pray again and you will instantly awaken in the pureland.

Wherever you go, whatever you do, whatever happens to you, remind yourself that it's illusory. Practice recognizing, "This is a dream; there's nothing solid or permanent to this experience. This is the bardo." Pray to your object of faith that you will be liberated. If you establish this habit well before death, you will remember this meditation and prayer in the bardo.

You can evaluate what the probable strength of your meditation will be at the time of death by watching your dreams. If you remain in the clear light of the mind—no longer involved with ordinary dream phenomena, but resting in awareness of mind's true nature—your practice is very great and death will be a door to liberation. If you usually have dream recognition—if you are aware while dreaming that you're in the dream state—then when you encounter death you'll most likely maintain some control over the situation. If you are caught up in your dreams, responding, for example, to a dream-enemy with anger rather than compassion, your emotions may determine the nature of your after-death experience. If you are doubtful about your meditative capacity, now is the time to strengthen your spiritual skills through practice.

By preparing throughout your life—with contemplation of impermanence and the illusory, dreamlike nature of experience, prayer, development and completion stage practice, *p'howa,* and the Great Perfection practice of resting in awareness of mind's nature—you can transform the fear and anguish of death and dying into an opportunity for profound spiritual practice and ultimate freedom.

Part V

On the Vajrayana Path

21 *Guru Yoga*

The Buddha said, "Without the lamas, there would be no buddhas." Many of the Buddhist scriptures and commentaries state that before the advent of the teacher in one's life, not even the concept of enlightenment exists, let alone the determined search for it. All spiritual methods, from the initial steps of taking refuge and bodhisattva vows, come from the lama.

In one way, our fortune is great. We're living in an aeon blessed by the appearance of a thousand buddhas, of which the Buddha Shakyamuni is the fourth. But in another way, we're unfortunate, for none of these buddhas has manifested in our time. However, as the Buddha Shakyamuni passed into parinirvana and his retinue implored him to remain, he promised that in periods of spiritual degeneration he would appear as spiritual teachers, that the dissolution of his nirmanakaya form would not hamper his activity in any way; the benefit would be the same.

Relying on a teacher to achieve liberation is the essence of the practice called guru yoga. The Tibetan word for yoga is *naljor*. *Nalba* means "pure nature," and *jor* means "finding" or "making obvious." Through guru yoga the lama's realization of mind's pure nature dawns as realization in our own mindstreams.

The understanding in guru yoga that the lama is the union of all sources of refuge speeds our progress on the path. If we relied solely on the yidam, for example, we would reach our goal far more slowly. The meditational deity is only one of the outer, inner, and secret sources of refuge all contained in the body, speech, and mind of the lama.

The lama embodies the Three Jewels of Buddha, dharma, sangha; the Three Roots of lama, yidam, and dakini; the wealth deity; the dharma protectors; and the three kayas.

The mind of the lama, the lama's realization of absolute truth, is identified with the buddha principle of the Three Jewels. The speech of the lama embodies the dharma principle, the verbal transmission of the teachings that benefit all who hear. The body of the lama is the principle of the sangha and the enactment of virtuous activity leading beings to liberation.

In addition, the physical form of the teacher embodies the first of the Three Roots, the lama as the source of blessings. Though we don't have the karma to have received teachings directly from the Buddha Shakyamuni, the lama speaks as the Buddha would have spoken and uses the means to guide us that the Buddha would have used.

We receive the lama's blessings directly through empowerment, instruction, and guidance in our practice. The lama introduces us to the fact that cyclic existence is a state of suffering and to the necessity and pursuit of liberation from that suffering.

After hearing and applying the lama's teachings, we begin to experience renunciation: we turn away from thoughts and actions counterproductive to spiritual development and cultivate those that are productive. Where there was ignorance, we now have some understanding. Where there was only ordinary conceptual mind, we now taste awareness. Our pervasive self-interest and the poisons of the mind slowly diminish, and our capacity to deal with them increases. Our perception of the world begins to change. These are all blessings of the lama.

Just as the physical form of the lama embodies the root of blessings, so the lama's speech embodies the principle of the yidam as the root of accomplishment. The term for accomplishment in Sanskrit is *siddhi,* in Tibetan *ngodrup,* which means realization of the true nature of mind. So far, the only thing we have accomplished is the failure to recognize this nature and the perpetuation of the cycles of samsara.

The lama teaches us that the true nature of what we have accomplished lies beyond conventional reality. By ripening us through empowerment, freeing us through teachings, and sustaining our practice with blessings and inspiration, the lama enables us to experience directly the true nature of mind. Realization of that nature, not samsara, is the accomplishment we rightly seek. Yidam literally signifies "mental bond" or "mental commitment"—a commitment to listen to and apply unerringly the methods given us by the lama. By keeping this commitment, we realize the ultimate accomplishment. Thus we say the lama's speech, the lama's teaching, is inseparable from the yidam.

The mind of the lama embodies the third of the Three Roots, the dakini, the feminine principle of wisdom and the root of auspicious circumstances and enlightened activity. When awareness of the true nature of phenomena has become an ongoing state of realization, enlightened activities manifest without effort, as a natural outflow.

We usually refer to four kinds of enlightened activity: pacifying, enriching, the activity of power, and direct wrathful intervention. On the relative level, pacification means allaying one's fears and suffering. Enrichment means increasing one's merit, longevity, and health in this lifetime. Power means drawing together the necessary circumstances

to support spiritual development. Direct wrathful intervention means cutting quickly through obstacles on the
path.

Each of these activities also has a more profound function. The ultimate activity of pacification resolves the poisons of the mind in their own ground, including ignorance
concerning the nature of reality. Ultimate enrichment
brings the accumulations of merit and wisdom to fullest
possible expression. The ultimate activity of power involves
overcoming all confused and superficial thought patterns by
awareness of their true nature. Finally, ultimate direct
wrathful intervention annihilates all the ways in which we
invest things with a self-nature and solidity they do not
have; the sword of transcendent knowledge cuts through
and liberates ignorance.

The play or display of emptiness as form is referred to
in Tibetan as *tendrel,* "auspicious circumstances." Enlightened activities arise as the auspicious circumstances of
the realization of the dakini, of mind's true nature, embodied in the mind of the lama.

The teacher embodies yet another principle, that of the
wealth deity. In Vajrayana Buddhism there are both wealth
deities and wealth practices. Many people believe that if
they do such practices they will become rich. But actually
another kind of enrichment takes place: that of merit, aspiration, and spiritual qualities in daily life. One of the effects
of this practice may very well be material prosperity, but
that's only incidental to the major benefit of releasing the
mind from avarice and greed. The lama is the source of
methods by which we accumulate merit and break the tight
bonds of selfish desire and insatiability. This helps us to become free of both material and spiritual poverty. Thus the
lama is said to be inseparable from the wealth deity.

The lama also embodies the principle of the dharma
protectors, or, in Sanskrit, *dharmapalas.* The Tibetan term

for protector is *gonpo,* which literally means "friend," "ally," "someone who helps or benefits." Although traditional depictions of dharma protectors as wrathful and ferocious beings with large mouths, heads, and eyes have symbolic value, the underlying meaning remains that of an ally, the supportive influence of the teacher and the teachings. Ultimately, it is our own path of virtue that protects us from the suffering we would otherwise experience as a result of nonvirtue. But it is the teacher who instructs us in the consequences of nonvirtue and the benefits of virtue. The lama safeguards our dharma practice, protecting us from our misunderstanding of the teachings and from errors in our application of them.

Finally, the lama embodies the three kayas. The mind of the lama is dharmakaya, original purity beyond confusion and delusion. The lama's realization of the formless, substanceless nature beyond words is transmitted nonverbally from mind to mind. The speech of the lama is the sambhogakaya, that which is halfway apparent, intangible, benefiting beings through verbal communication. The physical body of the lama is the nirmanakaya display of enlightened mind, appearing in tangible form to show us the path, to guide and lead us to liberation.

We can't devise infallible spiritual methods on our own. Life is very short; we're subject to many illnesses and obstacles—we don't have time to waste reinventing the wheel. Nor can we learn these methods from books alone, for what we get from reading is highly subjective—we give it our own interpretation; a book can't offer us feedback like, "No, wait a minute, that's not what I meant," so we have no way of verifying our understanding.

Words and concepts simply can't liberate us, for they are part of the mechanism of dualistic mind. They can't give us a taste of mind's essence or lead us to its realization. Even the enlightened Buddha said, "Though I would think to say, there are no words." It is impossible, given the limitations of human intelligence and conceptual thinking, to communicate the ultimate truth verbally. Conceptual mind is bound by object–subject duality. But mind's true nature cannot be grasped dualistically; it's self-seen.

Though words can't catch the absolute truth, they can point to it. Like a finger pointing to the moon, the lama's words can indicate the right direction. Ultimately, it is the teacher's realization of the truth that catalyzes the awakening to our own intrinsic awareness.

Relating to a teacher is like plugging into an electrical outlet. If electricity is flowing, it will come directly to us. But if there isn't any electricity coming through, nothing will happen. This may not be the best of examples, but in a way it's a good one because we don't know exactly what electricity is. We only know what it can do. By relating to one who has a direct experience of the absolute truth, we can connect with that truth. The purpose of honoring, accepting, having faith in, and being receptive to the teacher, then, is to realize this truth ourselves, not simply to appreciate someone else's realization of it.

When our minds start to change as a result of the methods given us by the lama, we begin to recognize more and more of the lama's noble qualities, and our faith increases. When our faith meets the realization of the lama, the meaning of the absolute nature is born in our minds. It's a combination of the teacher's qualities and our own faith, prayer, and practice that liberates us.

Because the methods we use don't require proximity to the lama, we can practice guru yoga anywhere—even if the lama is no longer alive. If we have strong faith, we can pray to the lama in the morning about something we don't understand and gain some insight or resolution by the afternoon. This is because the lama's essence is wisdom realization. Wisdom, like the light of the sun, is all-pervasive, the same whether near or far. Though the sun sets, it doesn't stop shining.

Through our habit of dualistic perception, we build walls in basic space, creating artificial boundaries. But on the level of absolute reality, there is no separation, no near or far: the lama's wisdom is no different from that of all enlightened beings. This all-pervasive wisdom that lies beyond one or many, separate or together, is the absolute lama.

Through the blessings of the lama and the diligent practice of guru yoga, our realization increases and a profound faith grows that makes our eyes water, our hair rise. Our minds open to this same wisdom, blending in boundaryless space with the mind of the lama. This is the mind-to-mind lineage.

It is difficult to find a perfectly qualified teacher, but the one we choose as our guide on the spiritual path should at least have certain qualities. The teacher not only should know the literal meaning of the teachings but should have attained some direct realization of them. He or she should have the inner warmth of meditative insight, an energy that penetrates to the heart of the words. The teacher's practice should have reached a stage at which an indwelling confidence in the deeper meaning of the teachings and the dynamic energy of realization has been fully attained. Such a teacher's mindstream is filled with a spontaneous, unfabricated love and compassion for all beings. Seeing or hearing, even thinking about or touching that teacher is beneficial. His or her experience is so vast that it overflows to others.

A teacher like this is someone we call worthy of the title "lama."

The Tibetan word *lama* refers to two essential qualities: *la* means "high," in the sense of the most sublime realization of the nature of mind; *ma* means "motherly," referring to the quality of unconditional compassion that arises from realization. Although there are thirty attributes of a qualified teacher, if a lama meets this one crucial criterion of possessing motherlike compassion and has the student's interests completely at heart, then he or she will be of benefit. There should be no desire for fame, to have a large circle of followers—only a sincere wish to cause those changes in students' minds that will produce liberation.

Lord Buddha spoke of the 84,000 possible delusions and the 84,000 methods that antidote them. A spiritual teacher must be familiar enough with this vast system to find the method most suitable to each individual student. Moreover, the teacher should have a facility for working with people of different dispositions.

At the very least, a teacher should function like a doctor, not necessarily the best in the world, but a good one. Just as a competent specialist who treats only one type of disease can benefit those with that particular malady, a teacher whose knowledge and experience may be limited can still be beneficial.

Teachers need to be honest about their limitations. If they don't know something, they should say so. They shouldn't pretend they understand something they don't and thereby mislead students who believe in them. Many teachers make a big mistake in not referring students to someone else who can help them in a particular area or better meet their needs.

Teachers with pure intention will do whatever may prove necessary—nurturing, holding, protecting, or sending

students elsewhere, displaying peaceful or wrathful means
—without selfish concern. Teachers with altruistic motivation who speak only of what they understand, who maintain
dignity, integrity, and ethical behavior, benefit their students even if they don't possess all the ideal qualities of a
lama. If, however, a teacher lacks the pure intention of
bodhicitta, sooner or later someone will start to sense that
something is wrong. Tibetans say that you can wrap a dog
turd in beautiful brocade and for a while it will look lovely,
but sooner or later somebody is going to smell what's there.
Without pure intention, a person can act like a spiritual
teacher and perhaps bring short-term benefit to a few
people, but sooner or later the person's absence of qualities
will tell. Problems and difficulties will develop that make it
obvious something is awry. According to another Tibetan
proverb, falsehood goes only as far as a guinea pig's tail—
which means not very far at all. Truth, on the other hand,
is long lasting, like a valley you can walk through for days
without reaching the end. When a person's life is in harmony with the truth, positive qualities endure. Those who
pretend to be teachers, fooling themselves and others, have
as much to sustain their posturing as the length of a guinea
pig's tail. After a brief time they aren't convincing anymore.

Before we accept someone as our teacher, we must carefully examine his or her qualities and capabilities. Although
a false teacher may not have negative intent, to accept such
a person is like drinking poison. At the same time, for a
teacher to accept a student without examination is like
jumping off a cliff. The teacher has to determine whether
the student has correct motivation and intends to apply the
teachings as they are meant to be, without distorting or cor-
rupting them for some selfish purpose.

Once we begin to study with a qualified teacher, that
teacher becomes more important to us than the Buddha

Shakyamuni himself, even though the teacher's qualities could never excel those of the Buddha. This is because he or she is a living teacher, someone through whom we have direct contact with the dharma. The founders of our current healing tradition were very kind, but they are long dead. We get our medical care from living practitioners who uphold the long tradition of past healers. Likewise, the lama can help us in a more direct, personal way than the Buddha himself and therefore is regarded as even kinder than the Buddha.

The title "Rinpoche," Tibetan for "precious" or "of inestimable value," is sometimes applied to teachers because of the role they play in the lives of their students. The term comes from the Indian and Tibetan mythology of the wish-fulfilling gem, a gem that appears for the benefit of beings as a result of their collective merit and aspirations, one so magical that any wish made in its presence is fulfilled. The lama is like such a gem.

When we admire and respect someone as a teacher, we want to be like that person; we want to possess the same wonderful qualities. This inspires us to apply the teachings, confident that they will lead us to the same state the teacher embodies. The tantras say that to depend on the lama is to rely on all buddhas; to behold the face of the lama is to behold the face of one thousand buddhas. It is said that if one sees the lama as a buddha, one will receive a buddha's blessings. For if we understand that the teacher has all the qualities of a buddha, we will follow that teacher's guidance wholeheartedly until we attain enlightenment. If we have no faith or devotion, if we remain cynical or skeptical, we won't follow through with our practice and we'll never progress on the path.

Devotion to the lama, then, should not be thought of as excessive, mindless dedication to someone whose intention may be questionable, like that of a slave to a tyrant. Such an attitude isn't demanded of us. Rather, we feel devotion for the lama, physically, verbally, and mentally, not for the lama's benefit, not to please or make the lama rich, but because in this way we create receptivity and cause waves of blessings and merit to infuse our mindstream.

What we feel is based on a deep appreciation for what the teacher gives us. We understand that through the lama's compassion, realization, and blessings, as well as our own faith, devotion, and desire to emulate those qualities, we will experience the inseparability of our mind and that of the lama.

As soon as we start the practice of guru yoga, we begin to notice changes. We find that our negative emotions and confusion diminish and our positive qualities and realization increase. Our relationships improve; we are more calm and relaxed, less likely to get upset or argue with people. All of these tangible benefits reinforce our faith in the lama and the teachings. The more our faith increases, the more we feel the lama's blessings. This increases our faith even more, which increases the blessings, a process that continues until we reach a level of unchanging, incontrovertible faith. At that point our confidence is unshakable.

The relationship between student and teacher as the very foundation of the path must be properly understood. Though it's been subject to a great deal of misinterpretation, it isn't something new to Buddhism, not a recent innovation devised to draw in students, but rather a proven method of practice for highly realized practitioners and masters over thousands of years. The reason there are lineages of genuine spiritual teachings alive today is that practitioners, generation after generation, have gone through the process of finding a true teacher, relating to that teacher with devotion and respect, receiving spiritual transmission, gaining realization, and then joining the next generation of those who inspire respect and devotion in their students. That is how it has happened in the past, and it is clearly happening now. As long as there are people willing to devote themselves to benefiting others, and as long as there are those who can advise them on the means to do so, that is how it will continue into the future.

Question: In order to attain enlightenment, how much should we rely on ourselves and how much on the lama or some other external power?

Response: We need an element of both: we have to rely on something external as well as on our own efforts. Though we gain realization by our own efforts, the catalyst for this transformation is a relationship with a worthy teacher and the application of authentic teachings.

When we begin practicing, we look outside our own limited experience for the means to liberation; it's not sufficient to rely entirely on ourselves, because that hasn't worked in the past. If it had, we wouldn't still be wandering in samsara. None of us wants to suffer, and yet we do, despite our best efforts. So we need to look to something or someone who can show us the way beyond suffering.

At the same time, we rely on our own efforts by listening carefully to the teachings, contemplating their meaning deeply, finally internalizing them through meditation. So in the final analysis, it is mainly through our own practice that we accomplish our goal. Success lies, in a sense, in the very palm of our hand.

Question: You referred to the lama's mind as the dakini, but I thought that the dakini is a female deity.

Response: Dakini refers to the feminine principle of wisdom that manifests in female form to benefit beings. We say the lama's mind is the dakini because it embodies the inseparability of emptiness and wisdom, the absolute dakini. This absolute nature, dharmakaya, manifests as the subtle display of the sambhogakaya dakini and the nirmanakaya physical form of great female realization holders in order to benefit beings.

Question: Is it more beneficial to study with one lama or with many?

Response: The teacher is like a doctor, and the practice is like medicine. You don't go to a doctor to benefit the doctor; you go because you need to get well. Though many doctors may be highly recommended, there is no point in visiting them all or, without knowing any of them well, mixing the medications they prescribe. Similarly, there is no reason to shop for spiritual teachings without ever fully applying any one of them.

If after following a doctor's treatment plan carefully, you experience some improvement, you can supplement this regimen with that of a specialist. Similarly, after choosing a reliable teacher, you may want to supplement his or her teachings with those of another lama.

If, however, you go to a second doctor who isn't as skillful as the first, his or her diagnosis might directly conflict with the first. Then the second doctor's medicine will negate whatever good has been done, and your health will deteriorate. You may receive from one lama teachings on compassion and the four thoughts. You might then go to another teacher who tells you that you don't need to do the preliminary practices. This will only undermine all the very good advice given by the first teacher. Even within the tradition of authentic lineage holders, there are teachers and there are teachers. A teacher–student relationship is like a mold: your realization will be only as great as your teacher's. Before you enter a relationship, make sure the teacher's qualities are ones you'd like to emulate.

Moving from teacher to teacher is like tearing seedling

after seedling out of the ground and planting a new one each time. Your practice will never have a chance to mature; you'll keep disrupting the continuity necessary to bear fruit. However, if throughout your practice, you maintain your commitment—in essence, the committment to reduce the mind's poisons and increase love and compassion—then receiving additional teachings from other lamas will be like adding water and fertilizer to the seedling. Then it will bear fruit.

If you're not benefiting from a particular teacher, there is no reason to continue studying with that teacher. Nor should a teacher try to hold onto a student anymore than a doctor should persist in treating a patient he or she can't help. It's better for the student to find a different teacher. There is no time in this brief human life to waste taking a direction that isn't productive.

Question: Could you say more about praying to the lama when we practice?

Response: Blessings arise naturally and our qualities increase like the waxing moon through prayer to the lama and by recognizing all aspects of practice—visualization, mantra recitation, and the dissolution of the visualization into emptiness—as the display of the lama's body, speech, and mind. With pure motivation and faith, we can swiftly accomplish the two stages of yoga—development and completion.

22 Introduction to Great Perfection

The teachings of the Great Perfection, or Dzogchen, the swiftest and most profound Buddhist path, are by tradition secret. They aren't freely revealed, because like snow lion's milk, they have to be held in a special container. Traditionally, the Great Perfection was presented only to people of the highest caliber, those almost awake. But such beings are very rare. Most of us need a developmental approach leading up to the teachings, for although we may be fortunate enough to have access to these teachings, we don't have the qualities or the aptitude to awaken effortlessly to mind's nature.

In order for the fruit, the state of great perfection, to become evident through practice, it is necessary to follow a complete path unerringly in a step-by-step progression. If you were to build a car, you'd be extremely careful to assemble every bolt in the correct way, to perfect every electrical connection, because otherwise the car wouldn't run. In the same way, you must take great care in developing your spiritual vehicle. For mere exposure to these teachings doesn't guarantee enlightenment. If the mind isn't prepared, the transformation that comes through genuine transmission from Dzogchen master to student won't occur. Just as a seedling requires certain conditions to bear fruit, we need to create conditions conducive to the full assimilation of the Great Perfection teachings. To do this, we use methods called the *preliminary practices,* or *ngondro,* to make ourselves purer receptacles. Then the Great Perfection teachings will have the fullest possible impact.

The requirements for receiving Great Perfection teachings are completion of the preliminaries and empowerment. The preliminary practices are like a bellows fanning the flames of a fire, causing it to blaze. These are not baby practices that we do only when we start out on the spiritual path. They're like the ABCs we incorporate into every aspect of our education. The preliminaries connect us to dharma just as our obscurations connect us to samsara; they purify those obscurations and enhance our understanding all along the way. They incorporate every method we need to reveal the mind's true nature.

We begin the preliminary practices with the four thoughts. People often think, "I've already heard the four thoughts." But in that case they've allowed them to become rote; they haven't penetrated to their meaning. These contemplations are essential to Great Perfection because they undercut samsaric attachment and engender enthusiasm for practice.

First, we contemplate the precious conditions we enjoy. These include the sacred spiritual methods available to us and the teacher from whom we receive them, as well as our human body with its unparalleled capacity for spiritual accomplishment. We realize that this cherished opportunity won't last. Once impermanence intervenes and we lose this life, our karma won't disappear. Whether it will lead us toward liberation or further samsaric suffering depends on our practice.

We make a commitment, then, to take full advantage of this opportunity, and we pray that we will accomplish our purpose. Then we drop all thoughts and allow the mind to rest, which permits our conceptual understanding to sink in and leads our practice in the direction of Great Perfection meditation.

We might begin by devoting 80 percent of our practice to contemplation, 20 percent to resting the mind. When we start to experience less negativity and more enthusiasm for meditation, we know the contemplations are permeating our consciousness. Then we can let the mind rest for 30 percent, 40 percent, 50 percent or more of the time.

We prepare ourselves further through the *extraordinary preliminary practices*. We take refuge in the teacher, teachings, and lineage lamas of the rare and precious Great Perfection, reiterating our bodhisattva commitment to follow in their footsteps along this extremely short path in order that all beings might swiftly awaken to the glorious state of the great perfection. In addition, we purify karma, gather merit, augment positive qualities, and rely with faith and devotion on the perfect teacher and teachings in order to deepen our awareness.

In my experience, there is a big difference in receptivity to Dzogchen teachings between one who has completed the preliminary practices and one who hasn't. There is also a difference between someone who has engaged in these practices diligently, with pure motivation and concentration, and someone who hasn't focused, who has simply counted mantra repetitions with a wandering mind.

In my area of Tibet, there lived a lama whose meditation seemed very good. He had done well in all the different steps of practice. But when it came to the Great Perfection, he simply couldn't understand the teachings—he hit a wall in meditation. So his teacher told him to recite the hundred-syllable mantra of Vajrasattva 10 million times. He went into retreat and practiced day and night for nine years. When he came out, understanding arose effortlessly.

What is the significance of the term "Great Perfection"—or "Great Completion," as Dzogchen is sometimes translated? What is it we call perfect, complete? The true nature of mind is original purity, complete in and of itself— it needs no enhancing. When one tries to look at mind, there is nothing to find. Those without view will discover nothing, nor will an enlightened being. Yet everything that arises is the play of mind, in no way separate from mind, just as waves are not separate from the ocean.

Within the nature of mind, samsara and nirvana are complete. Enlightenment itself is not beyond this nature. This completion—of all of samsara, of nirvana, of enlightenment itself—is the scope of Great Perfection. The *chen* of Dzogchen means "great," in that all beings throughout the three-thousand-fold universe have this complete, original purity.

If mind's true nature is complete or perfect, why do we suffer? Why do we need to meditate? We follow the path of Great Perfection because we don't see our perfection. Like heat melting ice, our practice dissolves the solid appearances of reality that obscure our essential nature, and the true qualities of mind become completely obvious.

So the *foundation* of Great Perfection is this great completion. The *path* is the process of removing that which obscures the foundational nature of mind. And the *fruit* is the complete realization of this foundational nature, fully revealed.

In the Great Perfection approach, since the path is forged of awareness itself, we must differentiate between ordinary mind and awareness. Our intrinsic awareness in the present moment, free of recollection or ordinary thought, of artifice or contrivance, is itself dharmakaya, the enlightened intent of original purity. This is directly introduced in the immediacy of our own true nature as self-occurring pristine awareness, or wisdom. Beyond the three times of past, present, and future, we come to a decision in the immediacy of this experience. Self-arising and self-freeing, like waves resolving back into the ocean, recollections and thoughts resolve into the ground of being, leaving no trace. We gain an inner confidence in the immediacy of this freedom.

When we are immersed in that unwavering state, our appreciation for and enjoyment of phenomenal reality enhance our realization, a process termed conduct. These and other aspects of this approach must be heard in more detail directly from a qualified lama.

The highest view must be combined with impeccable action. Then our practice becomes infallible. We can talk about buddha nature and emptiness, but if we haven't realized it, our words alone won't create transformation. We need to be very honest about our capacity. If we're a fox, we mustn't think we can leap as far as a lion, even if we can see the goal. If we don't have profound realization of the true nature of reality, we must be extremely careful in our actions. We can't discount our relative experience, thinking it doesn't matter because everything is empty. We must remain attentive to it until we attain enlightenment.

As practitioners we're very young, like kindergarten children. We mustn't drink poison, whether the nature of that poison is empty or not. We may be students of Great Perfection, but if our understanding is incomplete, our thoughts, speech, and actions negative, we'll still make negative karma; the Great Perfection won't liberate us. We'll just get more deeply entrenched in samsara. Until we have attained stable realization, everything we do, think, or say counts. The great master Padmasambhava said, "In my tradition, one's view is as high as the sky and one's actions as fine as barley flour."

Acting with great care, meditating, maintaining view brings maturity to practice and accelerates progress on the path. Shantideva said that if we know mind's true nature directly and maintain that knowing, all dualistic experience will be conquered and all poisons of the mind purified. If you are doing great practice, you'll notice changes day by day. If your practice isn't as effective as that, change will occur week by week, month by month, or year by year. If there is no change at all, even after years of meditation, the fault lies with the quality of your practice. You can't blame the dharma.

These days, although many people talk about Great Perfection, the level of realization isn't what it used to be. Not as many practitioners attain rainbow body, the dissolution of the body's elements into light upon the attainment of enlightenment. People say they're doing Great Perfection, yet haven't even accomplished the basics of reducing anger, attachment, and ignorance.

The problem isn't to be found in the teachings themselves. Nor has the mind-to-mind lineage been broken. It's that practitioners aren't diligent. One can't simply choose a teaching, practice as much of it as one likes, and ignore the rest. It doesn't work that way. It is essential to persist in one's efforts from the very foundation to completion.

We may receive great teachings and methods, but if we don't make use of them, we're like someone amassing money that won't go across the threshold of death—we're just wasting time. If we practice Great Perfection diligently, we can attain enlightenment within seven years; or with more diligence, purity, and receptivity, within three years or even one. Without such qualities, we can sit in retreat for sixteen or thirty-two years, our minds racing, and achieve nothing at all. Our retreat hut will only feel like a jail. Or we can practice in the midst of worldly activities, directing the mind to dharma, resting in awareness, each moment of the day, and attain enlightenment in this very life.

The bodhisattva undertakes effortful meditation and performs beneficial activities, though aware they are illusory, for the sake of those trapped by their belief in their seemingly solid reality. This leads to the fruit of the path: the full realization of one's foundational nature, the all-completing great perfection. Through the full accomplishment of view, meditation, and action, beneficial activity arises spontaneously.

23 Mind of Activity, Nature of Mind

In the Buddhist tradition, we distinguish between intellectual understanding, unstable experience, and stable realization. Intellectual understanding, like a poorly stitched patch that eventually falls off, is temporary. If we go further in our practice, we may have a glimpse of the true nature of mind, but like mist, it will dissipate. What we are working toward is an unalterable realization, like space itself, which by its very nature never changes.

When our understanding of impermanence and the illusory quality of existence increases, we begin to observe phenomena without projecting our false assumptions; with time, we come to recognize open, naked awareness as our true nature and the true nature of reality.

To get to this experience of what is natural, start by acknowledging impermanence in every action of your body, every word of your speech, every movement of your mind. As you move your hand, recognize the change in its position as a demonstration of impermanence. First it was on the left, then the right. With your breath, recognize impermanence as it comes and goes, comes and goes. With practice, the deliberate intellectual process of looking at each thing and thinking, "This is impermanent," evolves into a natural, uncontrived knowing of the ongoing display of change. This gentles our stance toward reality; we begin to appreciate the truth of the Buddha's metaphors describing phenomena as illusions or dream images, hallucinations,

echoes, or rainbows—apparent but not tangible or corpo-
real—like reflections of the moon in water, brilliant yet not
solid.

Our ordinary understanding is based on assumptions
that have been passed along to us, assumptions that depend
on ordinary ways of perceiving. We have been taught to
name things, investing them with a reality they don't have.
Ordinary mind is very linear, clicking through one thought
after another. We may believe we're multifaceted, mosaic-
like thinkers, but we're just very quick changers. All the
concepts and thoughts that arise in the mind, in fact, our
whole experience of reality, aren't much different than a
finger-drawing on the surface of water. Even as the image
is created, it's no longer there.

Belief in the solidity of experience produces attachment
and aversion, which in turn perpetually fuel the fire of samsara, until reality can seem a raging inferno. Understanding
the truth of our experience is like no longer putting wood
on the fire. The flames don't immediately disappear, but
without fuel, the fire slowly dies out. Without attachment
and aversion, we aren't confused by the push and pull of
phenomena. There in that natural openness—the clear
space of the mind at the end of a thought, before the next
arises—is awareness.

Great practitioners have attained enlightenment by continually bringing awareness to their work. All day long for
twelve years, the Indian master Tilopa pounded sesame
seeds to make oil. With each movement, his awareness re-
mained fully present; it didn't slip off into past or future,
into flights of imagination. The same was true of Togtzepa,
a practitioner who dug ditches; with each movement, he
maintained awareness.

Similarly, many of India's eighty-four *mahasiddhas*,
highly realized practitioners, worked at ordinary jobs. As

they labored, they meditated. It didn't matter what they did. By resting in awareness in the midst of their activities, they developed the capacity to transform fire into water, water into fire, to walk through walls and fly through the air. Rather than remaining subject to ordinary reality, they became its master. Of course, it's not the purpose of meditation to change water into fire. But such capacities are a natural by-product of cutting one's clinging to ordinary perceptions of reality.

Once a king's son went to a yogi for meditation instructions. After the yogi had shown him a method, the boy said, "This won't work for me. But I do know music. Is there a meditation I can practice while playing my instrument?"

"Remember as you play," the yogi replied, "that sound is emptiness and emptiness is sound. Sound is not beyond emptiness, emptiness is not beyond sound."

We, too, can change the mind swiftly if we bring awareness to all of our activities. When you build, keep your mind present with each movement of the hammer. Don't let thoughts intervene. As you write, keep your mind with each movement of the pen or stroke of the computer keys. Don't let it jump around. When you cut wood, maintain awareness with each strike of the ax. Whatever you do, relax the mind. It's a process of gently resting in openness, immersed in what's going on, fully present, but at the same time conscious of the display of phenomena. An adult watching children in the park never loses track of the fact that they're playing. The adult doesn't deliberately focus on their activities saying, "They're playing, they're playing, they're playing." But there's a recognition, a knowing, of that fact.

We often lose this relaxation of the mind when we're completely consumed by our work, for example, when we're so involved in writing we're almost inside the words. But in resting the mind, there's a bit more space. It's like being a little outside of what's happening, aware that it's a display, but without distancing yourself and establishing duality.

The lives of great practitioners repeatedly show that in order to maintain one's practice of the dharma it's not necessary to renounce the world. Nor is it necessary to renounce the dharma in order to maintain worldly involvement. It's possible to integrate both into a single life. Gradually, new priorities and a necessary balance will emerge.

In my time, I've witnessed four people attain rainbow body upon their death, and they didn't live in monasteries —they were householders. When I was twenty-two, I saw a person attain rainbow body and most people didn't even know he'd been doing spiritual practice. There's no need to make an outer display to succeed on the spiritual path. It's not the body we change to become enlightened—it's the mind.

You can adopt a hermit's life-style, give up your concern for food, clothing, wealth, friends, family, home, go off into the hills, and devote yourself entirely to formal meditation. That is one perfectly valid way to practice. But in Vajrayana there's another way. Your outer life remains business as usual. You don't leave home, you don't renounce anything, but you are never separate from virtue, never separate from dharma, from the intention to benefit, or from awareness.

Tilopa said to his student Naropa, "You are bound not by appearances, but by your clinging to those appearances, so cut through that clinging, Naropa." We are bound to samsara not simply because we have possessions, or high status, or friends, but because we cling to them.

Practice has to happen consistently right where the mind is active, right there with the experience of desire or anger or happiness, at each moment. Then your meditation and your work join—it's a kind of marriage. If you want swift results, it's not enough to meditate only an hour or two a day. Never think, "I'll work now and meditate later." Who knows if you'll live that long? The lord of death is hard to put off. When he comes to visit, he won't listen if you say, "I'm sorry, but I've been so busy, and now I need to meditate. Just give me a week, a month, or three years."

Through devoted practice, we develop the ability to transform negative conditions into supportive ones. Called "carrying adversity onto the path," this means not being obstructed, swayed, or overwhelmed by something, but seeing it as an opportunity to practice.

The entire phenomenal world then acts as a teacher helping us to develop skill in dealing with life. We can make everything that happens to us a part of the path. Trials become opportunities for practice because they force us to develop patience. We learn to accept adversities joyously because we understand that, when we suffer, we purify karma. A single headache can purify what would be hundreds of years of suffering in a hell realm. This doesn't mean we reject happiness; rather, we rejoice in it, dedicate our merit to others, and pray that their happiness will last.

Sometimes when they begin meditating, people tell me that it's hopeless, that their thoughts are impossible to control. I assure them that this is a sign of improvement. Their mind has always been unruly; it's just that they're finally noticing it. In the past, they've let it roam freely, following whatever stream of thought occurred. But now that they're more aware of what goes on in the mind, they can begin to change. You may complain that meditation isn't easy. But remember that you're leading your mind, like a wild horse, into the corral of awareness. You'll know that your practice is working if you're not so dominated by your emotions and confusion, if you bring to whatever you're doing, wherever you are, openness, relaxation, and compassionate intention, remaining aware of the play of the mind and of the nature of everything taking place around you.

Once a student who was having problems in meditation came to the Buddha. When the Buddha asked how he made a living, the man replied that he was a lute player. The Buddha asked, "When you string your lute, do you pull the strings tightly or do you leave them very loose?" The man answered, "Neither. If I tighten them too much or leave them too loose, I get the wrong tone. I have to strike a balance." He'd answered his own question about meditation. Whether in our practice or in our work, we need to maintain a balance—being neither too tense and attached, nor too loose and sloppy.

There's a story about a fine lama with a rather dense student who asked obvious questions but never quite understood the answers. One day the teacher, in great frustration, looked at him and said, "But you don't have horns"—meaning, "You're not a cow, you should understand what I say."

The student, still not comprehending, thought the teacher meant that he *should* have horns. Taking this to heart, he went into retreat, where every day he visualized having horns. Three years later, the teacher asked his attendant, "Whatever happened to that student of mine who wasn't very bright?" When told the student was in retreat meditating, the lama exclaimed, "How can he be meditating? He doesn't know anything. Bring him to me."

So a messenger was sent to fetch the student. Arriving at the retreat cave, he peeked through the little door and saw the student sitting there with a lovely set of horns. The messenger called, "Your teacher wants to see you; please come."

The student stood up to leave, but couldn't get those huge horns out through the small door. He told the messenger, "Please extend my great apologies to my teacher. I would come, but I can't get out of the cave because of my horns."

The teacher, on hearing this, said, "That's wonderful! Now tell him to meditate on not having horns."

Through the power of his concentration, the student removed the horns in seven days and returned to the lama. Once he'd received proper meditation instructions, he very quickly attained realization.

People give many reasons for not doing spiritual practice. Some say they don't believe the teachings; others feel they're not ready or that they don't have the capability. But this is a mistake. Whether or not we believe in samsara, this is where we are. Whether or not we believe in karma, we're creating it. Whether or not we believe in the poisons of the mind, they are there. What is the benefit of not believing in medicine? Whether we're ready to do practice or not, death and sickness won't wait. Why not prepare? Why not develop the capacity to help ourselves and others? We're ready to drink poison, but not to take medicine.

Not meditating once we've received teachings is like shopping for all our favorite foods, arranging them beautifully in the kitchen, and then not eating. We'll starve to death. Meditating is like eating: our pantry is full and we partake of what we've gathered.

Instead of telling ourselves, "I don't have time today, I'll meditate tomorrow. I don't have time this week, I'll do it next week. This is a busy year, I'll get around to it next year," we need to feel an immediacy about doing practice— right now, not just today, not just this hour, but this very moment.

Now I pray that each and every being's true nature be revealed, that we each see clearly our inherent truth and find liberation from the shackles of suffering and difficulty imposed by the limitations of our mind.

To this end, let us dedicate all the virtue of this teaching, of the changes we will make from having been exposed to these truths, and of changes others around us will undergo by having seen us enact what we have learned.

So it flows out, in rings of benefit.

Index